THE

GOLDEN

GATE

BRIDGE

TITLES IN THE BUILDING HISTORY SERIES INCLUDE:

Alcatraz
The Eiffel Tower
The Great Wall of China
The Medieval Castle
The Medieval Cathedral
Mount Rushmore
The New York Subway System
The Palace of Versailles
The Panama Canal
The Parthenon of Ancient Greece
The Pyramids of Giza
The Roman Colosseum
Roman Roads and Aqueducts
The Russian Kremlin
Shakespeare's Globe
Stonehenge
The Suez Canal
The Titanic
The Tower of Pisa
The Transcontinental Railroad
The Viking Longship
The White House

BUILDING
HISTORY
SERIES

THE
GOLDEN
GATE
BRIDGE

by James Barter

Lucent Books, Inc., San Diego, California

Library of Congress Cataloging-in-Publication Data

Barter, James, 1946–
    The Golden Gate Bridge / by James Barter.
        p.   cm. — (Building history series)
    Includes bibliographical references and index.
Summary: Discusses the construction of the Golden Gate Bridge
and the people who designed and built it.
    ISBN 1-56006-856-6
    1. Golden Gate Bridge (San Francisco, Calif.)—Juvenile
literature. [1. Golden Gate Bridge (San Francisco, Calif.) 2.
Bridges.] I. Title. II. Series.
    TG25.S225 B37 2001
    624'.5'0979461—dc21

2001000068

Printed in the U.S.A.

CONTENTS

FOREWORD

Throughout history, as civilizations have evolved and prospered, each has produced unique buildings and architectural styles. Combining the need for both utility and artistic expression, a society's buildings, particularly its large-scale public structures, often reflect the individual character traits that distinguish it from other societies. In a very real sense, then, buildings express a society's values and unique characteristics in tangible form. As scholar Anita Abramovitz comments in her book *People and Spaces*, "Our ways of living and thinking—our habits, needs, fear of enemies, aspirations, materialistic concerns, and religious beliefs—have influenced the kinds of spaces that we build and that later surround and include us."

That specific types and styles of structures constitute an outward expression of the spirit of an individual people or era can be seen in the diverse ways that various societies have built palaces, fortresses, tombs, churches, government buildings, sports arenas, public works, and other such monuments. The ancient Greeks, for instance, were a supremely rational people who originated Western philosophy and science, including the atomic theory and the realization that the earth is a sphere. Their public buildings, epitomized by Athens's magnificent Parthenon temple, were equally rational, emphasizing order, harmony, reason, and above all, restraint.

By contrast, the Romans, who conquered and absorbed the Greek lands, were a highly practical people preoccupied with acquiring and wielding power over others. The Romans greatly admired and readily copied elements of Greek architecture, but modified and adapted them to their own needs. "Roman genius was called into action by the enormous practical needs of a world empire," wrote historian Edith Hamilton. "Rome met them magnificently. Buildings tremendous, indomitable, amphitheaters where eighty thousand could watch a spectacle, baths where three thousand could bathe at the same time."

In medieval Europe, God heavily influenced and motivated the people, and religion permeated all aspects of society, molding people's worldviews and guiding their everyday actions. That spiritual mindset is reflected in the most important medieval structure—the Gothic cathedral—which, in a sense, was a model of heavenly cities. As scholar Anne Fremantle so elegantly phrases it, the cathedrals were "harmonious elevations of stone and glass reaching up to heaven to seek and receive the light [of God]."

Our more secular modern age, in contrast, is driven by the realities of a global economy, advanced technology, and mass communications. Responding to the needs of international trade and the growth of cities housing millions of people, today's builders construct engineering marvels, among them towering skyscrapers of steel and glass, mammoth marine canals, and huge and elaborate rapid transit systems, all of which would have left their ancestors, even the Romans, awestruck.

In examining some of humanity's greatest edifices, Lucent Books' Building History series recognizes this close relationship between a society's historical character and its buildings. Each volume in the series begins with a historical sketch of the people who erected the edifice, exploring their major achievements as well as the beliefs, customs, and societal needs that dictated the variety, functions, and styles of their buildings. A detailed explanation of how the selected structure was conceived, designed, and built, to the extent that this information is known, makes up the majority of the volume.

Each volume in the Lucent Building History series also includes several special features that are useful tools for additional research. A chronology of important dates gives students an overview, at a glance, of the evolution and use of the structure described. Sidebars create a broader context by adding further details on some of the architects, engineers, and construction tools, materials, and methods that made each structure a reality, as well as the social, political, and/or religious leaders and movements that inspired its creation. Useful maps help the reader locate the nations, cities, streets, and individual structures mentioned in the text; and numerous diagrams and pictures illustrate tools and devices that bring to life various stages of construction. Finally, each volume contains two bibliographies, one for student research, the other listing works the author consulted in compiling the book.

Taken as a whole, these volumes, covering diverse ancient and modern structures, constitute not only a valuable research tool, but also a tribute to the human spirit, a fascinating exploration of the dreams, skills, ingenuity, and dogged determination of the great peoples who shaped history.

Important Dates in the Building of the Golden Gate Bridge

1849
An epidemic of gold fever swells the population of San Francisco.

1920
A feasibility study recommends construction of the Golden Gate Bridge.

January 5, 1933
Construction of the Golden Gate Bridge begins.

1872
Charles Crocker submits plans and cost estimates for a bridge spanning the Golden Gate.

1930
Joseph B. Strauss submits his final plans for the Golden Gate Bridge to the District Board of Directors.

June 1933
The north pier is completed.

1850   **1900**   **1930**   **1935**

1869
Joshua Norton calls for the construction of bridges crossing the bay.

1916
James H. Wilkins, a structural engineer, recommends the first serious design for spanning the Golden Gate.

February 1933
The anchorages are completed.

1923
The state legislature passes the Golden Gate Bridge and Highway District Act of California into law.

March 1934
The south pier repair is completed.

May 1934
The north tower is completed.

Workers inspect a catwalk during construction of the Golden Gate Bridge.

January 1935
The south pier is completed.

June 1935
The south tower is completed.

March 1936
The suspension cables are completed.

One of the "Seven Wonders of the Modern World."

February 16, 1994
The Golden Gate Bridge is named one of the "Seven Wonders of the Modern World" by the American Society of Civil Engineers.

April 1937
The deck surface is completed.

May 27, 1937
The Golden Gate Bridge opens to pedestrians.

| 1935 | | 1940 | 1980 | 1999 |

February 22, 1985
The one billionth car crosses the bridge.

August 1935
The catwalk cable is installed.

May 28, 1937
The Golden Gate Bridge opens to vehicles.

May 24, 1987
The Golden Gate Bridge celebrates its fiftieth anniversary.

May 1936
The cable compression is completed.

March 1999
The Golden Gate Bridge is awarded the number-two position in the Top 10 Construction Achievements of the Twentieth Century.

September 1936
The roadway steel is completed.

INTRODUCTION

The Golden Gate Bridge, known simply as The Bridge by local San Franciscans, is a central part of this glitzy cosmopolitan city. Life without it is inconceivable. Spanning the Golden Gate, the entrance to the San Francisco Bay from the Pacific Ocean, this red steel arc carries thousands of daily commuters between San Francisco and its northern neighbor, Marin County.

Although the Golden Gate Bridge was built to carry commuters, its importance to residents of the Bay Area goes far beyond being simply a stretch of freeway. The bridge is also a favorite destination on weekends for many San Franciscans who jog, walk, and bicycle across it. Boaters use the bridge as a navigational reference point and for leisurely weekend outings. Painters, photographers, and poets flock to the bridge to capture special colors, angles, and thoughts. Nearly all San Franciscans take pride in their bridge and easily understand why it is featured so frequently in dozens of movies and television series.

Before the beginning of the bridge's construction in 1933, residents and visitors alike considered the Golden Gate to be one of the great natural wonders of the world. Tidal currents, gale-force winds, and the silvery fog of the Pacific surge through this mile-wide opening to the San Francisco Bay. A narrow slice in the coastal mountain range, the Golden Gate is a portal of unparalleled majesty and beauty through which many generations have sailed in search of better lives, including refuge from suffering, escape from poverty, and the freedom to pursue happiness.

However, critics believed that spanning the rough seas of the 1.2-mile-wide Golden Gate would be an impossible engineering feat and dubbed it "the Bridge that could never be built." Because of the climatic conditions in the Golden Gate, a bridge that could withstand the battering of waves, relentless winds, and San Francisco's infamous earthquakes was needed. To overcome these obstacles, engineers devised revolutionary techniques for steel assembly, underwater concrete construction, and cable design. Never before had a suspension bridge of this length been attempted, nor had anyone ever tried to build a bridge in open ocean waters.

Constructed during the Great Depression, when most families had little money and the unemployed sometimes outnum-

Many San Francisco residents are proud of the Golden Gate Bridge and everything it represents.

bered those who were employed, the Golden Gate Bridge became a symbol of hope. Construction companies hired thousands of workers to build the world's longest bridge. As the twin towers pierced the San Francisco sky, local residents as well as seamen from foreign ports marveled that a structure of this size could be built during these economically tough times. The Gateway of the West, as it is known, has been more than a symbol for optimism in times of depression. It is also a place where thousands of appreciative confetti-throwing Americans welcomed home transport ships of soldiers following World War II, and has served as a gesture of friendship extended to foreigners who still look to America as the land of opportunity.

In fact, the Golden Gate Bridge is San Francisco's most recognized work of architecture. Universally acknowledged as the most revered, most recognized, and most photographed bridge in the world, it is also the most visited monument in the United States. To San Franciscans, "the Bridge" is not simply a bridge; it is an art form, considered the city's most beloved sculpture and America's most significant landmark. Chosen in 1994 by the American Society of Civil Engineers as one of the "Seven Wonders of the Modern World" (second only to the Chunnel running under the English Channel), the Golden Gate Bridge demonstrates a rare combination of function and beauty. It is a superb example of what can be achieved by giving ordinary human effort a direction and a purpose.

THE BRIDGE THAT COULDN'T BE BUILT

The earliest reference to the Golden Gate occurs in 1846, four years before California became a state, when John C. Fremont and a renegade band of Americans sought to take control of California from Mexico. In the process of crossing the bay in a canoe to attack a Mexican fort at the 1.2-mile-wide strait leading from the Pacific Ocean entrance to the San Francisco Bay, Fremont is said to have named it *Chrysopylae*, the Greek word for "golden gate."

At that time, the San Francisco Bay was sparsely populated and the thought of bridging the Golden Gate for commuters would have seemed ludicrous. Unbeknownst to Fremont, however, that idea was not far off. Two years later, in 1848, the discovery of gold dramatically increased the population of the San Francisco area, and the need for a bridge would soon become a reality.

BEFORE STEEL

Northeast of San Francisco, a three days' journey by horse leads to the foothills of the Sierra Madre mountain range. Here, in 1848, legendary stories were told of miners becoming instant millionaires upon discovering veins of pure gold. As exaggerated reports of gold spread throughout America and later the world, ships loaded with enthusiastic miners sailed for the closest port to the gold fields: San Francisco. In little more than a year, the population of San Francisco exploded from three hundred to thirty-five thousand residents, and many new cities sprang up around the perimeter of the bay.

Traveling between the many new cities of the bay was not a simple undertaking. Small wooden ferryboats transported early settlers between Marin County to the north and the East Bay cities of Richmond, Berkeley, Oakland, and San Francisco. As

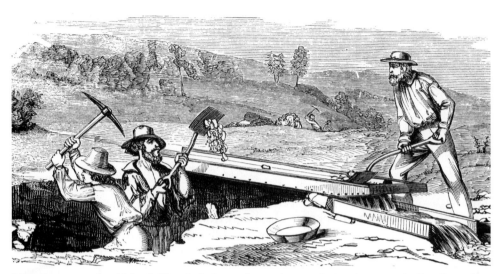

The discovery of gold in California led to a dramatic population increase in San Francisco and the other cities surrounding the bay.

the numbers of commuters grew and delays became common, many wished for faster and more reliable travel. A few began to speak openly about bridges that could connect the cities around the perimeter of the bay.

CALLS FOR A BRIDGE

Entrepreneur Joshua Norton was one of the earliest people to imagine a bridge large enough to carry travelers across the bay. Norton came to San Francisco from London with a small fortune and a large vision of becoming a multimillionaire. During the gold rush, there was money to be made supplying the tens of thousands of miners flocking to San Francisco from all over the world. Selling miners tools, clothes, and food, Norton's entrepreneurial spirit rapidly earned him a reputation throughout San Francisco as the most successful speculator in land, buildings, food, and mining materials. In a few years, he was not only one of the wealthiest men in the city but the most colorful. A bizarre character with a knack for unpredictable behavior, Norton had lost every dime by 1853. Destitute, alone, and increasingly eccentric, he declared himself emperor of the United States.

As a result, when he wandered into the office of the *Oakland Daily News* on August 18, 1869, with a drawing of an idea about building three bridges around the perimeter of the bay, few people took him seriously. He recommended what is today the Oakland Bay Bridge, the Golden Gate Bridge, and a third bridge (which has never been built) out to the Farallon Islands. Historians recognize Norton as the first person to call for the building of the Golden Gate Bridge.

THE 49ERS

In January 1848, in the little town of Coloma, California, not far from Sacramento, James Marshall discovered gold at Sutter's Mill, changing forever the history of California. Although Marshall initially discovered only four nuggets, the largest a mere quarter ounce, he knew the significance of his find and tried to keep the strike a secret. News of the discovery, however, quickly spread to San Francisco, then throughout America, and finally around the world. The exclamation of "Eureka," the Greek word for "I have found it," became the cry of the day for successful gold miners. Later, Eureka became the state's motto and the name of a city in Northern California.

Driven by hopes of buying a farm or paying off a large debt, the men struck with gold rush fever who flooded to California in 1849 were dubbed the "49ers." Ready to greet these men in San Francisco and the California gold fields were unscrupulous merchants eager to charge them inflated prices for supplies. Newspaper articles from this era record businessmen buying up every mining tool imaginable, including shovels, mining pans, and picks. After they cornered the market on these tools, they raised their prices to astronomical heights, forcing newly arrived miners to pay up to $15 for a mining pan that the merchants had bought for 50 cents a few days earlier. Many businessmen pocketed far more money than the miners did.

The population growth in San Francisco alone exploded overnight from a village of three hundred people to a metropolis of thirty-five thousand and became the focal point of world attention. This population boom, combined with increased wealth, brought California into the Union in 1850 and assured its future prosperity. The gold rush continued for several years before the rich veins were depleted.

Pictured is a view of San Francisco Bay before the construction of the Golden Gate Bridge.

Norton's idea of spanning the Gate was not the crackpot idea that many San Franciscans at the time believed. Just three years later, in 1872, Charles Crocker, the multimillionaire owner of the Central Pacific Railroad, met with the Marin County Board of Supervisors to present his plans and cost estimates for building a bridge across the Golden Gate.

Crocker had a driving passion for performing engineering feats viewed by most people as impossible. He had supervised the building of the western leg of the Transcontinental Railroad that ran through and over the treacherous Sierra Nevada. Dynamiting through granite mountains and building wood trestles across river gorges was standard fare for this engineering dynamo. Crocker saw how the railroads had opened up the West for millions of Americans moving away from the old industrial cities of the East in search of new opportunities. With its population of 300,000 and growing, Crocker decided to extend his railroad into San Francisco.

After the completion of the Transcontinental Railroad extending from Sacramento to Omaha, in 1869, San Francisco continued to grow. The World Exposition in 1894, drawing more than 2.5 million visitors, established San Francisco as the jewel of the West Coast and as one of the great cosmopolitan centers of the world. Thousands continued to flock to San Francisco and neighboring cities such as Berkeley, home to one of the world's great universities. The need for a bridge to move commuters around the bay was becoming increasingly apparent.

However, Crocker had been dissuaded by his friends, who viewed the bridge as a wild idea, and by his colleagues. Part of the resistance to Crocker's and Norton's ideas stemmed from the lack of engineering expertise at the time: Engineers did not believe that they had the materials or knowledge required to build a 1.2-mile bridge over turbulent ocean waters. In 1916, however, James H. Wilkins, a newspaperman who held an engineering degree from the University of California at Berkeley, became the third man to propose the construction of a bridge. Unlike his predecessors, Wilkins was able to address most of the engineering problems associated with building a bridge.

As a civic leader, Wilkins also believed that as the population of the Bay Area increased and the automobile became more of a necessity than a curiosity, such a bridge would be necessary. In 1910, 44,000 automobiles in California shared the mostly dirt and gravel roads with horses; ten years later, 600,000 cars were driven on cement and asphalt streets; by

Charles Crocker's idea of a bridge spanning the Golden Gate was quickly rejected due to the lack of engineering knowledge at the time.

1930, that number had swelled to 2,195,520. Wilkins had statistics to support his interest in the bridge, but he lacked the political support needed to convince politicians that the time for the Golden Gate Bridge had arrived.

To generate public awareness, Wilkins stated the following in his San Francisco newspaper, the *Bulletin*:

> It is possible to bridge San Francisco Bay at various points, but at only one such point can a bridge be of universal advantage—at the watery gap, the Golden Gate. . . . To begin with, the enterprise should appeal to San Francisco with overwhelming force. The northern coast counties . . . are growing faster, on the basis of merit alone, than any other part of Northern California. Nothing can be more important to San Francisco . . . than the speedy development of the region whose business comes to it automatically. And nothing can hasten that development more effectively than opening them to the free circulation of modern life by a bridge across the Golden Gate.[1]

ENGINEERS AND AUTOMOBILES

Michael M. O'Shaughnessy, San Francisco's city engineer, read Wilkins's article in the *Bulletin* with interest. As a senior engineer, he had managed the building of the Hetch-Hetchy system of dams and aqueducts built to carry water 156 miles from Yosemite to San Francisco. O'Shaughnessy saw the merit of alleviating the traffic jams at the San Francisco ferryboat wharves and became the first to actively promote the bridge. However, before action could be taken on Wilkins's proposal, the United States became embroiled in the First World War in 1917 and all discussion turned to Europe.

THE BRIDGE THAT COULDN'T BE BUILT

Following the end of World War I in 1918, America returned to the normalcy of peacetime life, which allowed many civic leaders to again recommend building bridges across the bay. O'Shaughnessy viewed the Golden Gate as a natural place for a bridge. Just 1.2 miles across, this narrow gap between the low coastal mountain ranges to the north and south seemed to be an excellent bridge location.

O'Shaughnessy took control of the venture from Wilkins and polled several of his colleagues about the feasibility and cost of spanning the Golden Gate. With the exception of a couple of people, most responded negatively; one person thought it was possible but believed that the costs could exceed $100 million. Many respected bridge builders and engineers had good reasons to doubt the feasibility of spanning the Golden Gate. In fact, there were more reasons not to build the bridge than there were to move forward with the project.

Opposition to the bridge was led by Bailey Willis, a noted Stanford professor of engineering. Willis believed that no bridge

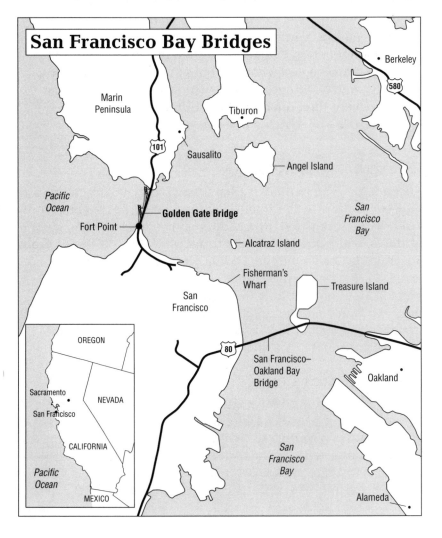

could span the distance proposed for the Golden Gate Bridge, and on many public occasions he simply said that it couldn't be built. Up till this point in time, the longest bridges in the world were hundreds of feet shorter than what would be required at the Golden Gate. In fact, it would be more than ten years before the George Washington Bridge would be built in New York with a record-breaking main span of thirty-five hundred feet, seven hundred feet shorter than what would be needed to bridge the Golden Gate.

Engineers opposed to the construction of the Golden Gate Bridge argued that no bridge could span the proposed distance.

In addition to the concerns about the incredible length of the span, the earthquake of 1906 was still fresh in the minds of San Franciscans. Many people remembered with horror the destruction of tall buildings and ensuing fires in the downtown section of San Francisco. Geologists studying earthquakes knew that slippage along the San Andreas Fault, just twelve miles east of San Francisco, had caused the earthquake. Many wondered what would have happened if the bridge had existed at that time. Others asked engineers if they could guarantee the safety of such a bridge if another, even stronger earthquake should strike the area.

Most pessimism, however, stemmed from the local knowledge of the exceptionally difficult geography and meteorological conditions of the Golden Gate. High winds, surging currents, daily tides, high waves rolling in from the Pacific, and dense fog combined to create one of the worst possible places to build a bridge. These conditions often caused ships to smash against the rocks and sent others to the bottom of the bay. Doubts that a bridge could withstand nature's conditions were not surprising.

THE BATTLEGROUND

Most of the surging water activity at the Golden Gate is the result of the daily tidal ebb and flow. Benign swirls and rivulets at the surface mask deeper currents propelling one-sixth of the volume of the bay through the Gate each day. At the rate of 2.3 million cubic feet per second, it is three and a half times the volume of water that the Mississippi River disgorges into the Gulf of Mexico. When the tide is at its crest, the volume doubles and moves with such power that swimmers and surfers can lose their lives in the turbulence as they are sucked under and out to sea.

The tides exert the greatest force on the waters of the Gate, but other natural forces add to the treacherous conditions. Forty percent of California land drains its melting winter snowpack into the bay. Many rivers also empty into San Francisco Bay, contributing to its turbulence. Annually, these rivers disgorge billions of cubic feet of water, creating a volume that exceeds the rampaging Colorado River at its flood level. Hundreds of feet below the surface, the fresh water of the rivers collides with the salt water of the Pacific. This collision causes a massive volume of water to be pulled through the narrow opening to the bay, creating a powerful surge.

Water was not the only climatic concern voiced by the critics of the bridge. Winds blowing up to eighty miles an hour, although infrequent, were another concern. These winds not only could twist a bridge into life-threatening angles but could cause it to collapse. Combined with the currents and tides of the deep water, the winds can churn the surface of the bay into fifty-foot killer waves pounding and vibrating the piers of a bridge.

A fourth climatic condition that posed a threat to a bridge was the fog. Famous throughout the world, the fog has earned San Francisco the nickname "Fog City." Although it is not a force that affects the water, fog regularly hides the Gate from view, causing ships to collide with rocks and with other ships passing through the narrow opening. Seasoned bridge builders were also concerned with the additional dangers that the damp, cold fog would bring to crews working high above the water.

JOSEPH STRAUSS

In 1870, Joseph Strauss was born in Cincinnati, Ohio. At an early age, Strauss showed an unusual interest in the bridges that spanned the meandering Ohio River. In his later life, Strauss would remember spending his childhood lying in bed watching the glow of the gaslights on one of the nearby bridges.

Born with a quick wit and a proclivity for mathematics and science, Strauss was senior class president and received high marks in high school. When asked what he wanted to do when he graduated, he said that he wanted to do something no one else had ever done before. After high school, he entered the school of engineering at the University of Cincinnati. While at the university, Strauss earnestly pursued bridge engineering and traveled to many cities to inspect their bridges. For his graduation paper, required for an engineering degree, Strauss designed a bridge that would span the fifty-mile Bering Strait between Alaska and Asia.

Following graduation, Strauss worked for several prominent bridge-building companies. However, he failed to find the satisfaction he needed to keep his interest in bridge building sharp, and so he eventually founded his

"I CAN BUILD IT"

Considering the difficult conditions at the Gate, it is easy to understand why so many believed that the Golden Gate was a poor location for a bridge. Despite the problems, the bridge remained a possibility because of the need to relieve commuter congestion. One engineer named Joseph Strauss believed that not only was the bridge feasible but he could build it for between $25 and $30 million. Strauss was a bridge builder who earned distinction around the world for many of his bridge construction projects. Considered by his peers to be a brilliant innovator, Strauss had built a favorable reputation for accepting challenges others thought to be impossible. In fact, Strauss was one of the engineers O'Shaughnessy had consulted. His parting comment to O'Shaughnessy was "I can build it."[2]

O'Shaughnessy and Strauss presented drawings and studies to the San Francisco Board of Supervisors that detailed innovative

own company. After completing his first bridge over the Cuyahoga River in Ohio, he earned a reputation as an innovative bridge builder.

Over the next several decades, Strauss built more than forty bridges around the world. A fiercely competitive man quick to criticize others and reluctant to share credit with his colleagues, he fiercely pursued answers to challenging engineering problems. He gained a mystique for dreaming large dreams and solving engineering problems thought unsolvable by his colleagues. Strauss was well suited for the job of building the Golden Gate Bridge.

A statue of Joseph Strauss stands near the Golden Gate Bridge.

design ideas for safely spanning the Golden Gate. Strauss's design addressed all climatic conditions and proposed sound engineering solutions to all of them. As a result, the board endorsed a survey to determine the feasibility of bridging the Gate. The feasibility study, completed in 1920, found that a bridge was not only possible but highly practical for moving the growing mobile population. In May of that same year, the California legislature voted to form the Golden Gate Bridge and Highway District to thoroughly investigate all aspects of the proposed bridge site.

However, the plan faced immediate opposition. Its biggest critics were the independent ferryboat companies and the railroads that owned many of the ferryboats; both groups stood to lose millions of dollars if commuters had faster, cheaper, and more reliable access to San Francisco and Marin County. The ferryboat companies had invested huge amounts of money over

A ferryboat crosses the Golden Gate. When automobile use increased, ferryboats were redesigned to accommodate them, but traffic jams at wharves soon emerged.

the years building long piers into the bay and purchasing boats large enough to carry automobiles.

Moving San Francisco's ballooning car population around the cities of the bay was not an easy task because it required crossing the water. Hundreds of ferryboats operated on the bay carrying residents to and from San Francisco. In 1917, this fleet of ferries carried 43 million people across the bay. However, as the use of automobiles increased, ferryboat designs changed to accommodate cars. In 1928, ferryboats carried more than 2 million cars across the Golden Gate. As a result, traffic jams began to emerge. The worst congestion occurred at the ferryboat wharf in Sausalito, just north of the Golden Gate. On sunny weekends, thousands of cars lined up for the ferry trip across the Gate to enjoy the many scenic picnic areas in Marin County.

The opposition on the part of ferry owners was understandable. Debates and public hearings took place throughout the Bay Area. Strauss himself went from city to city dismissing the interests of the ferryboat lobby with this standard disdainful observation:

> The ferry is at best a primitive and crude device. In the jungles of South Africa and South America and in every Sleepy Hollow Village we find ferryboats. It is incongruous in any other place.[3]

AESTHETIC CONCERNS

Opposition came from other groups besides the ferryboat owners. Longtime residents were concerned that the intrusion of a massive steel bridge would ruin the aesthetic beauty of the world-famous Golden Gate. Many residents who enjoyed the beautiful sunsets through the Golden Gate worried that a bridge would ruin this experience. Strauss attempted to calm their fears by publishing his drawing of the proposed Golden Gate Bridge in the local newspapers.

The public hated it, and the outcry against his design was thunderous. The design, which was not the bridge we see today, had heavy steel bracing in a crosshatched pattern that gave the proposed bridge a dark, heavy, unattractive profile. The general view of the citizens was that it was ugly and would be a blemish on the pristine Golden Gate.

In keeping with its reputation as the artistic and cultural center of the West Coast, San Franciscans demanded an elegant

The Golden Gate Bridge's art deco design is most prominently displayed on the towers.

bridge befitting the Golden Gate's natural beauty. Supporters and critics alike knew that a bridge spanning this natural opening to the bay would be viewed by all Americans as the gateway of the Pacific. Every bit as distinctive as the Statue of Liberty in New York Harbor, the bridge needed to form a dramatic and majestic entry to the bay.

The public condemnation of his design, combined with a genuine need for a first-rate engineering partner, motivated Strauss to hire a chief design engineer. Strauss chose Clifford

Paine, an East Coast engineer with a superb reputation as a bridge designer and construction supervisor. Paine looked at Strauss's bridge design and, in agreement with the public outcry, saw it as visually unappealing. It was Paine who designed the bridge that we see today.

Consulting architects Irving F. Morrow and his wife, Gertrude C. Morrow, joined Paine on the project and contributed the art deco style that already dominated the New York skyline on several Manhattan skyscrapers. This architectural style, which gained popularity in the 1920s and '30s, is recognizable by its sleek streamlined forms. The art deco style conveys elegance and sophistication by using simplicity, repetition, and geometric patterns. The two most notable art deco features of the Golden Gate Bridge are both found on the towers. One feature is the wide vertical ribbing on the four horizontal tower bracings, or portal struts, that are famed for catching the sun's rays. The other feature is the rectangular towers themselves that decrease in width as they rise, which emphasizes their height. The Morrows also added several secondary art deco features such as the pedestrian railing and the light posts.

The new architects and their new designs resolved most of the aesthetic concerns about the bridge. Finally, the structural engineers were able to focus their attention on the difficult task of figuring out how to build a bridge that would stand and service the commuters of the San Francisco Bay Area.

2

ENGINEERING A DREAM

Successful construction projects, large or small, all follow a similar process, and the building of the Golden Gate Bridge was no exception. Before the first bucket of cement could be poured, before the first rivet driven, and before the first cable slung across the Gate, the tough mental work of the engineers had to be completed, carefully checked for errors, and then checked again.

THE ENGINEERS

The engineering work required to design a bridge the scope of the Golden Gate demanded a team of men and women with a keen understanding of mathematics, physics, building materials, and the geography and climate of the location. Joseph Strauss acted as the chief engineer of his large staff, but he relied heavily on their ability to perform all of the calculations needed to design a bridge that would meet the needs of the community and, most important, not fall down.

The engineer most trusted by Strauss was Clifford Paine, but more engineering horsepower was needed. To his growing staff of engineers, Strauss added Charles Ellis, a man known for his bridge experience. Ellis had a long career building bridges as well as teaching bridge design at the university level. He worked with Paine to calculate the required tonnage of steel, concrete, and wire; the environmental effects of the winds, earthquakes, and ocean currents; and the effects of stress on parts of the bridge as they expand and contract with the daily changes in temperature, wind, tidal surges, and moisture. To calculate all of the variables, Ellis relied heavily on several branches of mathematics, including geometry, calculus, and algebra.

THE WORST POSSIBLE SCENARIO

One of the first and most important safety questions an engineer must ask is what are the worst conditions that could possibly impact the bridge at any single moment. Among engineers,

Clifford Paine (left) and Joseph Strauss were just two of the engineers who worked on the construction of the Golden Gate Bridge.

this is called designing for the worst possible scenario, and it occupied the thoughts of the engineering team for many months. They set themselves to the task of addressing the unique personality of the Gate in terms of the geography and forces of nature.

To survive a worst possible scenario, engineers designed the bridge to withstand ninety-mile-an-hour gale-force winds, weight on the roadway equivalent to bumper-to-bumper traffic, tidal surges of 4.6 million square feet per second, and an earthquake measuring 8.0 on the Richter scale—all at the same time. Although these conditions have never occurred simultaneously, it remains a possibility.

On many occasions the public voiced its concern for safety, prompting Strauss to answer questions of structural dependability this way:

> If the entire 4,200 feet of suspended span were jammed with loaded limousines standing bumper to bumper in all six traffic lanes; if the $10^{1}/_{2}$-foot sidewalks on both sides were crowded their full length with foot passengers standing shoulder to shoulder; if a 90 mile an hour gale . . . should suddenly press against the huge exposed side of the bridge, and if at that moment someone should saw both cables half-way through—why, the Golden Gate Bridge would stand.[4]

Although winds and tidal currents concerned engineers and citizens alike, fears of earthquakes headed their list of concerns. San Francisco has a long history of violent earthquakes, and the thought of a bridge toppling into the bay along with hundreds of cars was very disturbing.

EARTHQUAKES

San Francisco is subject to many forces of nature, but none instills sheer terror like an earthquake. Striking without warning, most earthquakes are small and go unnoticed by San Franciscans, but every thirty or forty years a "big one" strikes, such as the infamous earthquake of 1906 that was still fresh in the minds of many people. In an earthquake, buildings vibrate off their foundations—called footings by engineers—and are sometimes known to actually "walk" away. The fear that one or both of the huge bridge towers might "go for a walk" terrified many residents,

THE EARTHQUAKE OF 1906

On April 18, 1906, a tremendous earthquake centered in the San Francisco area rocked Northern California. Hardest hit was the city of San Francisco. When the earthquake struck the city at 5:15 A.M., hundreds of buildings in the downtown area either partially or entirely collapsed. Fire broke out shortly after the earthquake, and by 9 o'clock much of the city was engulfed in flames that leaped from block to block. Water pressure to the hoses was too low to douse the flames, and fire departments were unable to do more than wait for the fire to burn itself out. San Francisco was devastated more by the ensuing firestorm than by the earthquake itself.

By nightfall, 300,000 people were homeless. Feeding and sheltering the refugees became the city's highest priority. Eighteen thousand people found shelter in tents and shacks made from packing boxes. They cooked their meals at the relief committee's outdoor camps.

San Francisco's growing population quickly rebuilt the city by replacing many of the collapsed buildings with new and more beautiful ones. San Franciscans also learned that they would need to be vigilant about building large structures in an area prone to continuing earthquakes. In fact, a lot of the opposition to the building of the Golden Gate Bridge stemmed from the 1906 earthquake.

The earthquake of 1906 completely devastated San Francisco.

and more than one geologist forecasted the collapse of any bridge built in the Gate.

Strauss's senior engineer, Charles Ellis, when asked what would happen in an earthquake if one of the towers were to sink six inches or "walk" sideways six inches, replied, "Nothing." The reason why nothing would happen, he explained, was that the towers would sway without snapping and the cables would stretch to compensate for the tower sway. When asked how the bridge would survive a "big one," Ellis had this quip to silence the fears of San Franciscans:

> If I knew that there was to be an earthquake in San Francisco tomorrow and I couldn't get into an airplane and had to remain in the city, I think I should get a piece of clothesline about 1,000 or 2,000 feet long, and a hammock, and I would string it from the tops of two of the tallest redwoods I could find, get into the hammock and feel reasonably safe. If the bridge were built at that time, I would hie [hurry] me to the center of it, and while watching the sun sink into China across the Pacific, I would feel content with the thought that in the case of an earthquake, I had chosen the safest spot in which to be.[5]

Ellis was not the only engineer on Strauss's staff to face cross-examination on the topic of earthquakes. Charles Derleth, addressing the prestigious Commonwealth Club in San Francisco, dramatically underscored the threat of earthquakes. He stressed that more attention had been paid to earthquake-proofing the bridge than to earthquake-proofing any of the skyscrapers in the city. He stated to the audience, "If, because of an earthquake, the bridge were to fall, you won't care. There will be nothing left."[6]

A PLACE TO STAND

After addressing countless civic and government groups regarding the safety of the bridge, Strauss was eager to start the real engineering work of determining the precise place where the bridge would stand. Strauss and Paine had determined that two massive concrete piers to support the two steel bridge towers would need to be constructed on the watery floor of the Golden Gate.

The relentless daily surging of water in and out of the Gate for thousands of years had sculpted the floor in the shape of a gentle V with a maximum depth of 387 feet. Engineers needed to find two rock-solid moorings in the ocean floor to secure the concrete piers. To guarantee solid moorings, Strauss needed to find bedrock under the surface of the 1.2-mile channel that was capable of withstanding not only the weight of the towers—44,000 tons each—but also the 61,500 tons of main cables. Any substance other than bedrock would be too soft and the force of the currents would undercut the piers, causing them to sink under the intense weight.

In August 1929, marine engineers conducted a survey of the Golden Gate's channel floor. Borings, holes drilled into the ocean floor, were made across the strait to determine the best locations for the two towers based on the composition of the floor. The survey confirmed the existence of bedrock capable of supporting the tremendous weight of the towers. The test on the south side of the channel detected bedrock on a shelf eleven hundred feet offshore that could support a sustained weight of thirty-two tons per square foot, enough for the tower. On the north side, they were fortunate to find bedrock in shallow water against the cliffs. Strauss was pleased with the find. It would, however, create one significant change to his plans. Rather than the four-thousand-foot span he had planned, he would need to extend the bridge to forty-two hundred feet—seven hundred feet longer than any bridge in the world at that time.

Locating the positions of the piers created the momentum for the rest of the project. The forty-two-hundred-foot-long center span, which is the section of roadway between the two towers, determined the dimensions of the towers, which in turn established the length of the cables. With this information and the worst-case-scenario calculations, Strauss and his staff were now in a position to determine what type of bridge would meet their needs.

THE DESIGN: A SUSPENSION BRIDGE

Strauss and his team of engineers had designed many types of bridges over the years, and long-span bridges had always been one of two types, either cantilever or suspension. The cantilever bridge is recognizable by its spider web crisscrossing steel

The needed bridge length, the deep water of the channel, and the harsh winds that whip through the Gate ruled out the use of a cantilever bridge (pictured).

supports and its suspension section in the center supported by two towers. This design is very heavy and rigid and resembles the old-fashioned bridges designed during the late 1800s and early 1900s. In high winds, the cantilever design stands rigid, running the risk of actually blowing over or cracking.

A suspension bridge, on the other hand, has a much lighter look. Instead of the heavy crisscrossing of steel braces, a suspension bridge has two main cables strung over two towers to support the roadway. In high winds, a suspension bridge is designed to sway and then return to its normal position without structural damage.

The primary considerations that drove Paine toward constructing a suspension bridge were the extraordinary length of the bridge, the deep water of the channel, and the harsh winds that regularly whip through the Gate. Suspension bridges are typically found spanning deep water or gorges that slice through mountains. Since the Golden Gate is a very deep water channel, the suspension bridge was the only design that could possibly span the 1.2-mile distance. Design engineers chose the suspension design because it could sway in heavy winds rather than snap, as a cantilever would. Of the largest bridges in the world, the nineteen longest employ the suspension principle.

HOW A SUSPENSION BRIDGE WORKS

True to its name, the roadway in a suspension bridge suspends or dangles from the main cables that extend from one end of the

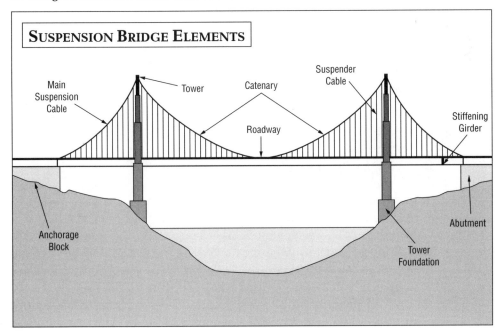

SUSPENSION BRIDGE ELEMENTS

THE HISTORY OF SUSPENSION BRIDGES

The most primitive and simplest form of the suspension design can still be found today spanning gorges and narrow rivers in many remote areas of the world. Built to carry only the weight of foot travelers, they are generally lightweight, narrow, and use woven vines as the two main cables. Once these vine cables are knotted to trees on opposite sides of a gorge or river, a walkway composed of wood boards is tied to the main vines. In this simple yet efficient way, remote people, using the same fundamental design that Strauss and his staff chose, have solved the problem of crossing difficult terrain.

Relatively few improvements were made to the primitive suspension bridge until iron and other forms of metal were invented. James Finley, an American, built the first metal suspension bridge in 1796. His longest bridge, in Philadelphia, was 306 feet long and made with iron chains. It was not until the mid-1850s that the earliest suspension bridges using cables were built in East Coast cities. With the revolutionary advent of the steel cable, longer spans were built rapidly. At the time the Golden Gate Bridge was conceived, the longest suspension bridge was the George Washington Bridge in New York with a center span of 3,500 feet.

bridge to the other. The Golden Gate Bridge, like all other suspension bridges, is simply a road suspended in the air. From the standpoint of the physicist or the engineer, bridges differ from the millions of other roads crisscrossing America in that they are built to defy gravity.

Suspension bridges, whether large or small, require the same five basic structural elements: the roadway, suspender cables, main cables, towers, and anchorages. All of these elements, much like the major elements of other structures, must be assembled in a logical sequence to counteract the force of gravity. Of these five elements, four are dedicated to the support of the roadway. In fact, the roadway is entirely dependent on the four, while they are entirely independent of the roadway.

The primary engineering principle at work in a suspension bridge is weight transfer. In its simplest form, a suspension

The George Washington Bridge in New York, an example of a suspension bridge.

Although the Golden Gate Bridge was the longest suspension bridge in the world when it was completed in 1937, several now exceed it. For instance, the Akashi Kaikyo Bridge in Japan, built in 1998, links the islands of Honshu and Shikoku and has a total length of 2.4 miles and a center span of 6,529 feet.

bridge transfers the weight of the roadway and vehicle traffic first to the suspender cables, then to the main cables, to the gigantic towers, and finally to the anchorages. The engineering trick to accomplishing this weight transfer is to design all structural elements perfectly.

CABLING

A huge pair of suspension cables holds the roadway high in the air. Flexible main cables, often the most noticeable and most dramatic of the structural elements, are secured at each end of the bridge by massive concrete anchorages. From each anchorage, the cables rise up to the tops of the two towers and then dramatically plunge down to the roadway in the center. The downward curve, or arc, that the cables form as they drop down from the towers is called a "catenary."

A catenary is the natural curve formed anytime a flexible chain or cord is held at its two ends. The two main cables of the Golden Gate Bridge must have flexible properties to form this catenary or the design fails. If each of the main cables was one monstrous solid strand, it would lack the ability to properly curve. To achieve the needed sweep of the catenary as well as the needed strength, engineers specified that each main cable must be made of thousands of individual steel wires bound tightly together. Steel, which is very strong under tension, is an ideal material for cables; a single steel wire, only 0.2 inches thick, can support more than one ton of weight.

The roadway, unlike the graceful sweep of the main cables, must remain flat to accommodate the flood of traffic on the bridge. To maintain this flat profile, suspender cables spaced every fifty feet connect the roadway to the curve of the main cables. Connecting a flat surface to a curved one requires many different lengths of suspender cables. The suspender cables at the bottom of the catenary are only a few feet long, while those near the towers, at the highest points of the catenary, are hundreds of feet long. Although the roadway is connected to the main cables by the suspender cables, what prevents the main cables from falling into the water?

ANCHORAGES

Concrete and steel anchorages attached at the ends of each main cable hold the main cables in place, along with the weight of the roadway and the commuting public. To hold the combined weight of the cables and the roadway, and to guarantee they will not collapse into the water, the anchorages are embedded in solid rock on both sides of the bridge. In addition, the anchorages must be heavy enough to counterbalance the weight of the cables and the roadway or the cable will collapse in the center, dragging the anchorages and the entire bridge into the water.

Inside the anchorages, thousands of individual cable wires within the two main cables are bundled into strands that flare out over a large area to evenly distribute the load. To prevent the bundles of wires from pulling out of the concrete anchorages, each strand is attached to one of the many huge steel holding pins embedded deep in the anchorages. With the cables firmly secured by the anchorages, what is the function of the steel towers that dominate the channel?

TOWERS

Many people think that the two colossal towers secure the main cables. It is easy to understand this misperception because the cables do indeed loop over the towers and exert tremendous downward pressure. However, the towers only provide the necessary height to create the arc of the main cables that support the roadway; they do not prevent their collapse.

Engineers must calculate the roadway's elevation above the water to ensure sufficient clearance for ships passing under the bridge. In designing the Golden Gate Bridge, Strauss initially believed that a two-hundred-foot clearance for ship passage would be sufficient for present and future needs. Ellis, however, reminded him that other modern bridges were already too close to the water to allow for the passage of modern ocean liners and warships. Strauss accepted this recommendation and increased the clearance at the center to 220 feet above the mean high tide.

The width of the towers was determined by the width of the roadway. Initial discussions for a train down the center and a double-deck design were abandoned for a single ninety-foot-wide deck without train tracks. Having established all critical dimensions and distances, Strauss could now accurately calculate the height of each tower at 746 feet above the water. Since the main cables would loop over the shoulders of the towers, Strauss designed the towers to lean and bend as the cables stretched and moved in the wind and changing temperatures. He calculated that the maximum side-to-side sway at the top would be 12.5 inches and a maximum back-and-forth motion of 40 inches. This need for sway necessitated further calculations for the structure and assembly of the tower sections.

Engineers Ellis and Paine designed the steel towers for flexibility, but they also designed them to attach firmly to the piers. Attaching steel to concrete was tricky—weight alone would not be sufficient. The solution was to use steel dowels or pins. As the pier forms were filled with concrete, steelworkers would set seventy-eight massive steel pins, 56 feet long and 6.5 inches in diameter, into the concrete. These pins were to extend 3 feet above the finished surface of the concrete and would mechanically lock the 746-foot towers to their piers.

Strauss calculated that each tower would stand 746 feet above the water.

SUGAR CUBES

To achieve the required strength and flexibility, the steel sections of the forty-four-thousand-ton towers could not be made of solid steel I beams. The structural engineers expended much brainpower to find a solution to this structural dilemma. They applied complex algebraic models before finding a simple solution that proved to be a stroke of genius.

Instead of designing towers made of solid, heavy steel I beams, they designed a basic 42-inch hollow cube made from ⅞-inch-thick steel plates that looked like an oversized sugar cube. Similar in concept to children's building blocks like Legos,

GALE-FORCE WINDS

All of the engineering calculations used to design a safe bridge were untested until February 9, 1938. On that day, seventy-eight-mile-per-hour winds whipped off the Pacific and were funneled through the Golden Gate, striking the western side of the bridge. In the early afternoon, Russell Cone, one of the engineers on Strauss's staff, drove on the bridge to observe how it was responding to the pounding. He observed that the entire length of the center span roadway was pushed to the side eight to ten feet from its normal position and that the winds were holding it at this slant. In addition, Cone noticed that the roadway was undulating about two feet every three hundred feet, giving the bridge a rippling effect similar to a rope or whip being cracked. However, the bridge directors did not close the bridge.

Cone later filed a report noting his observations and recommended that engineers review the possibility of adding more trusses to stiffen the roadway. The members of the Golden Gate Bridge Board of Directors refused to make Cone's report public, fearing the reaction to the potential problems with the bridge.

However, on three later occasions the bridge did close. As gusting winds reached sixty-nine miles per hour on December 1, 1951, the bridge was closed for three hours. During the closing, the bridge whipped up and down just under eleven feet, and light standards along the rail, set thirty-two inches apart, scraped paint off of each other. On December 23, 1982, seventy-mile-per-hour winds closed the bridge for almost two hours. The most recent closure on December 3, 1983, closed the bridge for the longest period in its history, three hours and twenty-seven minutes. Wind gusts reaching seventy-five miles per hour racked the bridge, but as had been the case before, it suffered no structural damage—and Charles Ellis was vindicated.

tens of thousands of these steel cubes became the basic units for constructing the twin towers. Hundreds of cubes were to be riveted together to form large sections of various sizes depending on where they were placed. The largest section would require 900 cubes, measuring 7 by 10 by 45 feet, and would weigh 85 tons. As the towers were to be assembled, each section would be placed in the appropriate location and then riveted together.

THE CENTER SPAN

Once the engineering team had found the sugar cube solution for tower construction, they set to work on algebraic calculations to account for the tremendous lateral forces against the center span that would result from the strong winds that blow in from the Pacific Ocean. These ninety-mile-per-hour winds have been known to rip a bridge apart. Strauss and his team recognized the need for a center span that would sway in the wind without snapping. After performing their equations, they found that they could design a center span capable of withstanding the worst storms. They calculated that a ninety-mile-an-hour wind would cause the roadway to flex up and down in a whiplike motion a total of 16.6 feet and sway back and forth 27.7 feet.

Once the tens of thousands of engineering hours had been completed and carefully reviewed, mathematical calculations cross-checked, and environmental assumptions confirmed, the moment of truth had arrived to implement Strauss's grand design. Fifteen years after Strauss first confidently proclaimed "I can build it," his expertise would now be put to the test.

3

Deep Roots

Like trees, great engineering achievements are only as stable as their roots. When asked how long he thought his bridge would stand, Strauss replied, "Forever."[7] Strauss and his staff checked all of their calculations many times and knew where every component of the bridge would link into the earth. Long before the glamorous cables and towers could adorn the glitzy San Francisco skyline, the dirty, sweaty work of preparing the earth for the bridge's foundation awaited the bridgemen who would spend the next two years living in mud and concrete.

The Anchors

On the cold winter day of January 5, 1933, the first shovels full of dirt were turned, inaugurating the start of the Golden Gate Bridge. Although this marked the actual start of construction, there were no ceremonies or long-winded speeches by politicians. Those would come later. Enormous steam shovels began the monotonous job of digging the four massive pits designed to hold enough concrete to anchor the north and south ends of the two main bridge cables.

The steam shovels dug into the earth down to an average depth of eighty-one feet. The depths varied from pit to pit depending on the geology. The total amount of earth removed was about 3.25 million cubic feet of dirt and rock—the equivalent of more than three thousand standard swimming pools. After clearing all the rubble out of the pits, carpenters built wood forms into which they would set reinforcement steel, called "rebar," before pouring the concrete. The forms were built as three separate interlocking sections extending down into the earth, acting like giant claws digging into the cliffs. This clawlike design helped prevent the anchorages from being dragged into the bay by the weight of the cables and roadway.

Enormous steam shovels were used to dig the pits for the anchorages.

Each of the anchorages was built in three interlocking steps. First, masons poured a rectangular base block 60 feet wide by 170 feet long and 97 feet high. This imposing slab filled all four of the pits well above the earth line. Set on top of these base blocks were anchor blocks that held sixty-one iron tie-down fixtures that would mechanically fasten the cables to the anchorages.

Workmen set the tie-downs into the cement when it was still wet. Each was forged in the shape of a giant sewing needle, 134 feet long, with a large round eye at one end called an eyebolt. When this phase of the pour was completed, only the round eyebolts protruded from the concrete. Three years later when the cables were actually locked into the eyebolt fixtures, the third and final pour would take place to completely cover the iron tie-downs and the cable ends. This last section added additional weight to the anchorages and provided security for the wires should anyone ever attempt to sever or bomb them. No such attempt has ever been made. When completed, each of the four anchorages would weigh 64,000 tons and be capable of resisting 32,500 tons of pull without budging so much as a millimeter.

CONCRETE WAR ZONES

The massive concrete pours appeared and sounded like a war zone. To ensure that the concrete would harden into a structurally solid mass, the workers poured the concrete twenty-four hours a day until its completion. If they failed to follow the continuous-pour policy, parts of the mass would prematurely harden, creating what mechanical engineers call "cold joints" between them. Those joined parts are not as strong as a single mass.

To fill the four anchorage pits with the necessary amount of concrete, engineers had to build special docks to accommodate barges carrying two thousand barrels of cement and five hundred tons of gravel at a time. Cement and gravel were unloaded from the barges and mixed with water in cement trucks to create the concrete. Revolutionary for the times, this was one of the earliest uses of cement trucks with large spinning barrels, which are commonplace today. The concrete was then driven to the anchorages and dumped down long chutes called "elephant trunks" into the pits. Once the trucks started coming, they didn't stop until they had filled the gigantic pit forms. The cement trucks with their barrels spinning on heavy chains, engines straining under the weight of fourteen tons of concrete, and brakes squealing on steep grades, sounded like tanks methodically, menacingly crunching their way down dirt roads.

The spinning barrels of the trucks prevented the concrete from hardening before reaching the pits. When several trucks choked the roads trying to get to the dump zones, the patience of the drivers and concrete workers could become frayed, and tempers often flared. If the trucks had to wait too long, the concrete hardened in the barrel and the drivers had to enter the barrel with jackhammers and chip it out—a hot, noisy, and filthy job no one wanted. Fistfights, although not tolerated by the companies, broke out from time to time.

While trucks brought the concrete to the pits, inside workmen sloshed about in the soupy wet concrete filling in the corners and packing it down so that no weak areas would later develop from air pockets. While some men pushed the concrete down with long pieces of wood that they worked like plungers,

After completion, each anchorage weighed sixty-four thousand tons.

Work proceeds on one of the anchorages at night. Lights frequently flickered and failed, making the pits even more dangerous.

others used steel electrical probes to vibrate the concrete into place. Whatever their job, the men's legs strained in the thick muck as if walking in quicksand.

Men working in the pits had to pay attention to the chutes that continuously funneled thousands of tons of concrete containing rock two to three inches in diameter. Sometimes the chutes would whip around and strike the men; other times men would get their legs caught in fresh concrete and couldn't free themselves. The fear of being buried in the cavernous cement pits was common, especially at night when lights frequently flickered and failed. Frenchy Gales, a concrete worker who poured the north anchorage, remembered one incident:

> I worked on a night pour at one of the anchorages. There were guys down in the cement. You'd walk on it to level it off. They took a count and we were short one guy. Everybody started stabbing around in the cement. We couldn't

find the guy. We had to notify his family. The timekeeper asked me if I would come with him. It was 1:30 in the morning. We went to his home. Knocked on the door. The guy answered in his pajamas. The timekeeper nearly fainted. The guy said, "I got tired. I went home and went to bed." That was the end of him on the bridge.[8]

THE NORTH PIER

Once the anchorages were well under way, the bridgemen turned to the two piers. The piers were enormous concrete blocks poured in the channel waters that would support the two steel towers. Strauss started with the north pier.

To get down to the bedrock lying many feet below the surface of the water, a cofferdam had to be set in place. Engineers had used cofferdams for years on structures in watery environments such as dams, locks, and bridges. Cofferdams are large four-sided boxes, without tops or bottoms, that are sturdy enough to resist the pressure of the surrounding water. Each of the four sides are steel sheets that are driven by pile drivers into the floor of the ocean so that the tops extend out of the water. This creates an enclosed box full of water. The box is then pumped dry to allow construction workers to work on the ocean floor in a dry environment safe from the obvious hazards of the sea.

Initially, leaks occurring along the corner seams were sealed with sacks of wheat that expanded in the water. Later, they used clay and dirt to stop the leaks. Dry and safe on the inside, diggers scrambled down the sides to begin excavating and found an unexpected treasure as described in Charles Adams's book *Heroes of the Golden Gate*:

> When the cofferdam was then pumped dry, to the delight of the men working on the project, the newly created floor looked like an open air fish market. Every type of fish and shell-creature flipped and slithered on the sea bottom, and they were theirs for the taking. Many a bridgeman's family ate a regal seafood feast that evening.[9]

Inside the cofferdam, the workmen dug down into the ocean floor using dynamite, jackhammers, pickaxes, and shovels until they hit bedrock twenty to thirty feet below the surface. After they had cleared out all of the rock debris, carpenters built a wooden form on top of the bedrock that would determine the final dimensions of the concrete pier. Steelworkers then entered the form and built a three-dimensional 107-ton grid of steel rebar to add strength to the concrete. Once the steel was set, concrete covered the reinforcement bars and filled the form to a height of forty-four feet above the water. The cofferdam was removed after the concrete had hardened.

The work was physically tough, uncomfortable, and filthy, but the idea of quitting to look for a better job was not an option because this was the era of the Great Depression when very few people could find work. Cement worker Frenchy Gales explained the employment situation to John Van Der Zee in his book *Gate:*

> The jobs, at least at this point on the bridge, were mostly unskilled and nonunion. There were other guys standing by the office waiting to go to work. You could see them, waiting to take your place. The pushers [foremen] wouldn't let you go to take a leak, have a smoke. If you did, you were gone.[10]

Once the concrete pour was completed, finish workers smoothed the expansive surface of the pier level to within a tolerance of $\frac{1}{32}$ of an inch by grinding it with a Carborundum® grinding wheel. Following this smoothing, they applied a specially prepared thick lead paste substance to the surface and polished it to a final base flatness within a tolerance of $\frac{3}{1000}$ of an inch. This attention to precision and detail was a hallmark of engineers Ellis and Paine, and it guaranteed a perfectly vertical tower. Both men knew that minor errors in calculations or overlooked environmental factors could place fatal stresses on steel and concrete.

Despite seemingly impossible standards, work on the north pier was completed by 90 construction workers in 101 days, two months ahead of schedule. The pier contained 23,500 cubic feet of concrete weighing 45,000 tons, an area larger than a 65-foot-deep football field. Flushed with a sense of invincibility, engineers and construction workers alike were giddy about taking on the south pier at Fort Point. None of them, not even Strauss himself, could have possibly imagined the anguish that awaited them 4,200 feet away.

THE GREAT DEPRESSION

The Great Depression was the worst economic slump in the history of the United States. It began in late 1929 and lasted until America's entry into World War II in 1941. One of the main causes of the Great Depression stemmed from the unequal distribution of wealth. A very small percentage of the population controlled most of the wealth and too many people bought goods on credit. However, it was extensive stock market speculation that led to the stock market crash of 1929 and the loss of billions of dollars of people's money.

Millions of Americans were unemployed during the Great Depression.

As a result of the crash, unemployment soared from 3.2 percent to 24.9 percent, leaving more than 15 million Americans out of work. Some remained unemployed for years. Those lucky enough to remain employed saw their income cut nearly in half between 1929 and 1933. Many during this period worked for nothing more than enough food to feed their families, while others left their families to look for work and were never reunited again. Many others could find only part-time work. For instance, one out of every four people in San Francisco was unemployed, and some were forced to sell apples and pencils on street corners to earn a little money. Others had to rely on food from soup kitchens set up by charitable organizations to provide at least one meal a day to the less fortunate. Lefty Underkoffler, a bridgeman, remembered the depression:

> In those days, a man's life wasn't worth a nickel, anyway. They figured one life for every million dollars on any job, no matter what type of work it was. In a time when [law]suits for negligence or personal injury were unheard of and men in the world outside were still standing in line for jobs, it was simple, practical bookkeeping for contractors to skimp on safety considerations in order to cut construction costs. The family of a fallen bridgeman would usually consider itself fortunate to be reimbursed for funeral expenses.

BUILDING A PIER ON THE OCEAN

The construction of the south pier was similar to the process involved in building the north pier. However, the south pier presented a greater challenge than the north pier because of its
location eleven hundred feet from shore and because the water
was deeper at this point than on the north side of the channel. It
was the first pier ever built in the open ocean, and it presented
Strauss and his staff with problems that they had not yet encountered.

Currents and winds presented a major difficulty. When the
Longyear Company originally tested the depth and composition
of the channel floor looking for good locations for the two piers,
they encountered dangerous currents. Stephen Cassady, in his
book *Spanning the Gate*, writes,

> The Longyear barge was moored with four 9-ton anchors
> and two 6-ton anchors, but still there were occasions
> when waves pitched the boat so violently that work had
> to be suspended for days at a time. It was as though Na-
> ture itself were opposed to the construction of the con-
> crete pier.[11]

Concluding that the work could not be done from anchored
barges, Strauss ordered the construction of an eleven-hundred-
foot dock stretching from Fort Point to the pier site. The dock
would provide access for workmen and heavy equipment.
Work on the dock began by lowering hollow cylinders to the
ocean's floor. Demolition experts dropped bombs through the
cylinders to blast holes for sixteen-inch steel I beams. Pile-
driving machines then pounded wooden poles deep into the
ocean floor. When these supports were in place, carpenters
built a temporary wooden roadway from the south shore out to
the pier site. By early August 1933, the finished dock included
electrical lines, telephone wires, a railroad track, a six-inch water pipe, compressed air lines, and room for heavy equipment.
Strauss, Ellis, and Paine were now prepared to begin work on
the south pier.

Work crews began assembling equipment for a cofferdam for
the south pier. The dangers of such an undertaking were numerous and extreme. The most obvious difficulty would be the
one-hundred-foot depth of the water at the pier site. Since it was

three to four times deeper than the north pier, the risk to deep-sea divers securing the cofferdam to the bedrock increased. Working inside of the cofferdam also had the potential for danger if a wall collapsed from the water pressure or if it was rammed by a freighter. Strauss knew that this would be dangerous because of the turbulence of the water and because his men would be working in the middle of a fog-shrouded shipping lane. When asked about the dangers of hard-hat diving, one veteran said in an interview with Stephen Cassady,

> That was okay with me. They'd pay me 25 bucks a dive, in addition to my salary. Hey, I needed the money. This was

FORT POINT

The international fame that the gold rush brought to San Francisco and California prompted an American military commission in 1850 to decide on the best defense for San Francisco Bay. The initial recommendation was to position a fort at Fort Point on the south side of the Golden Gate and at Lime Point on the north side. Each would be equipped with a battery of heavy cannons. With only one mile of water separating the two forts, military strategists speculated that any ship attempting to run through the defense would encounter a deadly barrage of cannon fire from both sides.

Between 1853 and 1861, the U.S. Army Corps of Engineers constructed Fort Point, which now sits directly under the south section of the Golden Gate Bridge. The fort was designed with 126 massive ten-inch Rodman cannons. Rushed to completion at the beginning of the Civil War, Fort Point was first garrisoned in February 1861 by Company I, 3rd U.S. Artillery Regiment. The fort at Lime Point was never built.

Fort Point was occupied throughout the Civil War, but the advent of faster, more powerful, and more accurate cannons made brick forts such as Fort Point obsolete. In 1886 the troops were withdrawn, and the last cannons were removed around 1900.

When early plans were drawn for the Golden Gate Bridge, Strauss recognized that the fort lay in the path of

the depression. My son had been born on the East Coast, and I hadn't paid for him yet. Those dives paid for my son.[12]

STRAUSS AT WAR WITH NATURE

On August 14, the freighter *Sidney M. Haupman*, outbound for Portland with a load of building materials, left from the East Bay port of Alameda. Steaming toward the fog-shrouded Gate, the ship drifted south, away from the safety of midchannel, and rammed through the dock 500 feet off Fort Point, creating a 120-foot gash. It left behind a trail of bobbing debris. The crash delayed work for a month while crews repaired the damage.

Protests from historians and community groups led to the preservation of Fort Point (pictured during the construction of the bridge).

the south end of the bridge. Some engineers recommended destroying the antiquated fort, but historians and community groups favored preserving it. Strauss and Paine found a solution. They designed a steel arch over the fort that supports the roadway as it passes overhead. The solution satisfied everyone, and today Fort Point offers one of the most unusual views in that it reveals the underside of the bridge to visitors.

This accident compounded the fear of a ship slamming into the cofferdam filled with workers. To protect the work site, Strauss and Paine designed a giant concrete elliptical fender around the pier site that would act as a permanent bumper. Designed to extend from bedrock to 15 feet above sea level, it would surround and protect the cofferdam from errant ships and the relentless pounding of the Pacific Ocean. The plan was to build the fender in twenty-two sections by lowering twenty-two steel baskets, each 30 by 35 by 20 feet, into place and then pumping cement into them underwater. After five baskets had been poured, nature struck again on October 24. Huge swells battered the dock and claimed three of the five fender baskets, the end of the dock, and all of the heavy equipment on it.

Strauss, a determined man whose personality was never to surrender, immediately repaired the dock and continued the

Determined to beat all odds, Strauss rebuilt the dock near Fort Point three times after storms and a freighter collision damaged it.

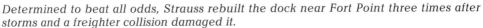

task at hand. He demonstrated a clear understanding of the obstacles when he said, "Building a bridge is a war with the forces of nature."[13] Six weeks later, in mid-December, the relentless power of the Pacific struck again with gale-force winds from the south. The fierce winds rolled the ocean surface into twenty-foot waves that ripped away eight hundred feet of the dock and then, almost as if taunting Strauss, claimed it by sucking it out to sea.

For a third time, Strauss ordered the dock to be rebuilt, but this time he raised a section of it five more feet above the ocean's surface to escape the crests of the waves. He knew that the pier was behind schedule, but the south pier could not be constructed without the dock. Workers once again rebuilt the dock, and in February 1934, eight months behind schedule, work resumed.

A BOBBING STEEL TOY

The rebuilt dock allowed Strauss and his crew to focus on completing the fender. Strauss finished the fender with the exception of one end that he intentionally left open. He designed the fender this way because he planned to float a large steel box called a "caisson" inside the fender instead of constructing a cofferdam.

The depth at which the construction workers could safely work warranted the installation of a caisson rather than a cofferdam. A caisson is a large steel box designed to protect workers at depths below seventy-five feet. Open at the top and bottom, like the cofferdam used on the north pier, the caisson's heavier steel sides provided workers with greater protection from the possibility of collapse. It also provided workers with oxygen, because at the depths at which they would be working fresh air does not easily circulate. When the pier was completed, the caisson would become a permanent part of the south pier. Similar to working in a cofferdam, workmen inside the caisson would smooth the bedrock, clear the debris, and set the rebar before pouring the concrete for the immense pier.

The plan was to tow the ten-thousand-ton preassembled 185-by-90-foot rectangle steel caisson to the site and place it inside the fender. Once in place, crews would then finish pouring the final wall of the fender and finally sink the caisson to the ocean floor. With the caisson in place, the final deep-water work could be safely completed.

THE FENDER

Builders of the Golden Gate Bridge feared that a ship might one day ram the south pier and cause massive structural damage. To protect the south pier, builders constructed a fender around it to act as a bumper. The fender was a major element in the building of the south pier. The size of an elliptical football field, 300 by 155 feet and 27 feet thick, it was a massive structure. The fender extended down to bedrock, 100 feet below the surface, and rose 15 feet above the water's surface. Demolition experts dropped bombs down tubes to blast away at the bedrock, on top of which the cement for the fender would be poured.

First, small bombs with three-pound dynamite charges were dropped into pilot holes that had been drilled. After placing about fifteen of these in each pilot hole, six large bombs weighing two hundred pounds each were lowered into the holes. Hard-hat divers then descended to attach detonating wires to them, and once the divers had surfaced the charges were detonated. The blasts were so strong that they caused the surface of the water to boil with dead fish. Hard-hat divers dynamited over a million and a half cubic feet of rock from the floor of the ocean. Large buckets were lowered to the bedrock and scooped up the debris. The process was repeated until the underwater shelf reached about thirty feet below bedrock. The sections of the fender were then put in place, bolted together, and filled with concrete poured from the surface.

Although Strauss and his engineers had perfected the workings of the caisson in theory, they had not yet gained a complete understanding of the ocean. On October 8, 1934, after three tugboats maneuvered the caisson inside of the fender, the captains tied their boats up for the night. The captains paid no attention to the gentle rolling swells as they fixed dinner. When coffee cups began sliding across their tables, however, their initial lack of concern quickly changed. The sounds of steel slamming into the concrete fender signaled a volatile situation. As the waves increased in size and frequency, the ten-thousand-ton caisson began bobbing like a toy.

Fifty-foot waves began breaking over the caisson, and the heavy steel mooring lines tied to the tugboats snapped like garden twine. Strauss and his lead engineers were summoned from sleep at 1:30 in the morning and converged on the site to decide

Fearing the massive damage that might result should a ship collide with the south pier, engineers constructed a fender around the pier to act as a bumper.

the best plan of action. As Strauss watched the caisson bashing the fender, he could see that both were being damaged. Sensing that the tugboats and their crews were now in danger, he hoped to save the caisson by pulling it out of the fender and towing it back to port for repairs.

Struggling to tow the caisson clear of the fender, the captains realized that they would never get it back to port safely. Acting on orders from Strauss and his staff, they dragged the sinking caisson into the Pacific and sank it with dynamite. Strauss now decided to proceed with the south pier without the use of the caisson. Thus far, nature was beating Strauss for control of the Gate.

Since the caisson would not be used, the fender was completed and would function like a cofferdam or caisson—as a form into which concrete for the pier would be poured. Before the pour began, engineers sank eight vertical hollow steel shafts four feet in diameter inside the fender down to the bedrock. These tubes would provide workmen with access to the bedrock.

Before further work on the pier could continue, the engineering team descended into one of the shafts to inspect visually, for the first time, the soundness of the bedrock. If it were not absolutely solid, the completion of the bridge would be abandoned, leaving the north pier as an everlasting tribute to the foolishness of underestimating nature. But for the first time in many months, luck was with Strauss as his engineers pounded on the bedrock with sledgehammers to test its durability. Jubilant about their findings, they were satisfied that the bedrock would hold the tower. When the pour finally began, the concrete teams filled the pier at the rate of one hundred cubic yards, the equivalent of fifteen truckloads, an hour.

To ensure that this pier would be precisely the same elevation as the north one, workers ground the base to the exact elevation that they had on the north pier. By January 3, 1935, Strauss had overcome the worst that nature could throw against him and the south pier was completed.

4

HIGH STEEL

Once the north and south concrete piers were completed they would be ready to support the steel elements: the towers, the main cables, and the suspender cables. Since Strauss needed to construct these components in a carefully orchestrated sequence in order to meet tight schedules and complete the project on budget, he actually started the steel construction of the towers prior to completing the piers.

SUPPLYING THE STEEL

An undertaking the size and scope of the Golden Gate Bridge included innumerable obstacles in need of resolution. The manpower needed to build the bridge was readily available, but the material was not. The many tons of high-grade steel required for the bridge could not be milled anywhere near San Francisco; all the big mills were located in the eastern regions of the United States. Strauss chose the Bethlehem Steel Company in Pennsylvania to manufacture and supply the steel.

The amount of steel ordered for the bridge was the largest order the company had ever received, and Bethlehem plant managers used four different mills to complete the job on time. Manufacturing steel far from the construction site generated concerns about how the steel could be shipped to California and what the bridge crews would do if the pieces didn't fit perfectly.

John Van Der Zee, in his book *Gate*, relates the importance of getting the right material:

> In consideration of any type of bridge, [Charles] Ellis [one of the lead engineers] explained, "the real test is not whether the structure can be designed nor indeed whether it can be fabricated in the bridge fabrication plants. The real test is whether the bridge, after it is fabricated, can be shipped piecemeal to the site and there be put together."[14]

Shipping eighty-eight thousand tons of steel was no small undertaking in 1933. Strauss and his engineers drew up a construction schedule that specified the sequence in which they would need specific types of steel and on what date they would

The Bethlehem Steel Company in Pennsylvania manufactured and supplied the steel used in the construction of the Golden Gate Bridge.

be needed at the San Francisco work site. Bethlehem Steel set its manufacturing schedule accordingly and arranged to have all parts shipped by train to Philadelphia, where they were then loaded onto freighters for passage through the Panama Canal and then on to San Francisco.

To guarantee that all the parts would fit perfectly once they arrived on site, Bethlehem Steel fabricated each piece with a stamped assembly number, punched all rivet holes in their precise positions, and assembled and then disassembled all pieces prior to shipping. The last job before shipping them to the West Coast was to apply three coats of thick lead paint to protect the steel from the corrosive effects of the salt air they would encounter in the Gate.

A similar problem occurred with the steel cable. The only company in the United States with the manufacturing capabilities of providing the cabling required for the bridge was the Roebling Steel Rope Company in Trenton, New Jersey. Strauss and his engineers calculated the sizes, lengths, and total number of coils needed, and the Roebling Company manufactured and shipped the steel through the Panama Canal.

ASSEMBLING THE TOWERS

The twin towers would be the first steel elements assembled. Impressive at 746 feet tall, when completed, they would be the tallest structures in San Francisco. Strauss decided to build one tower at a time rather than both simultaneously. Since both towers were to be identical, this was a wise management decision since he could save money by using only one set of cranes. An additional benefit would be that he would need only one crew, and they would work more efficiently on the second tower, having learned many lessons from the first. It was also a smart decision since pouring the south pier had fallen far behind schedule. Construction on the north tower began when the first steel shipment arrived from Pennsylvania in August 1933.

As the huge steel sections arrived in San Francisco, barges ferried them to the newly formed piers. A huge spider crane, named because of its ability to actually climb the towers, hoisted the numbered steel sections off the barge and hefted them into their predetermined places. The tower assembly was similar to putting together a puzzle with numbered pieces. Since all of the pieces of steel had been preassembled before shipping, the rivet holes of one piece generally lined up with the adjoining piece. However, at times, the ironworkers had to use pile drivers to hammer the steel sections until the holes were properly aligned. The riveting crews then permanently fastened them in place.

The legs of each tower were secured to the pier by the steel pins that had been embedded into the concrete. Once the legs of each tower reached the height of the roadway, 220 feet up, they were secured by X bracing below the roadway, where few people would see it, and by horizontal bracing called "portal struts" above the roadway, which would be in prominent view. This was more of an aesthetic decision than an engineering one because portal struts gave the bridge an appearance of lightness and elegance.

WALKING THE AIR

As the tower grew in height, the bridgemen hitched rides on the steel sections as the cranes lifted them. The men would often step from one steel section to another on their way up without safety lines or nets. This was known among the crews as "walking the air." Remarkably, none of the men died while performing these risky routines. The bridgemen didn't believe they were showing off or taking chances; they were simply moving around these gigantic structures in the most efficient way possible. Some men who found themselves near the tops of the towers at quitting time would actually slide down the outside of the towers, wearing leather gloves and using their boots to catch the rivet heads to slow them down.

Most of the tower assembly took place inside of the towers, where ironworkers and riveters worked using whatever light penetrated from above and the small lights attached to their hard hats. As the towers approached their 746 foot height, workers inside the legs could easily lose their way inside the maze of hollow sections. Many found themselves wandering for hours as they tried to find their way out at the end of the workday. This situation became so frustrating that a twenty-six-page map was finally distributed to the crews. Asked about the difficulty of navigating the interiors of the towers, Strauss once admitted that he doubted that he would be able to find his way out.

As the bridge builders worked their way to the top, a sickness broke out among the riveters. At first, one or two men complained

Workers were often said to be "walking the air" as they moved effortlessly between various steel sections of the bridge.

of headaches and stiffness in their joints. Shortly thereafter, dozens of riveters failed to show up for work, complaining about losing their hair and in some cases their teeth. Medical workers assigned to the health needs of the crews quickly realized that they had some sort of epidemic on their hands. It didn't take the doctors and nurses long to recognize that the illness was occurring inside of the tower maze and that the culprit was the lead paint applied to the steel in Pennsylvania. The white-hot rivets that the workers were setting in the steel caused the lead paint to burn, which sent poisonous fumes throughout the interior of the towers. Once the cause was discovered, engineers ordered a nontoxic paint to be used on the steel instead. None of the workers died from the lead poisoning, but it represented one of many unforeseen problems the bridgemen encountered.

On May 24, 1934, the spider crane hoisted the last steel cell of the north tower. With the exception of the toxic paint fumes,

THE MIRACLE OF STEEL ROPE

In 1831, John Roebling, an emigrant from Prussia, made his home near Pittsburgh, Pennsylvania, where he pursued his boyhood fascination with bridge building. Roebling found work as an engineer building dams and locks along the lengthy Pennsylvania canal system. Many years before the advent of motors, moving boats along the canals was done by horses attached to long ropes made from hemp fibers. Up to one mile long and eight inches in diameter, these heavy ropes continually broke under the weight of the boats, and repairs were timely and costly.

Roebling recognized that steel, a new material, might be a perfect replacement for the hemp ropes if it could be manufactured into a fine wire. In 1840 he produced and patented a six-hundred-foot steel wire, which he cut into several smaller pieces and then crudely wove together to produce the first steel cable. This new "steel rope" was one of the decisive breakthroughs in modern suspension bridge technology. Steel rope would allow bigger, longer, stronger, and more reliable bridges to be built.

Roebling began by building four small suspension bridges. In 1855, he built an 825-foot span across Niagara Falls for foot and carriage traffic. Bridge builders and engineers of every kind flocked to Roebling's new steel rope company to buy this revolutionary product.

the first of the landmark towers had proceeded almost flawlessly. Strauss had initially hoped to quickly complete the south tower after the north, but the problems he encountered pouring the south pier set his schedule back several months.

Riding an Earthquake

When the south pier was finally completed, the south tower went up faster and with even fewer complications than the north one. Since the two towers were identical, not much was different in their construction—with the exception of an earthquake that struck. Frenchy Gales, one of the bridgemen who was on the south tower when it struck, remembered the jolt:

In 1867, following the devastation of the Civil War, New York City contracted Roebling to build a great bridge across the East River to join Manhattan and Brooklyn. The sixteen-hundred-foot-long Brooklyn Bridge rising 130 feet above the water would accommodate millions of people and horses each year. One day while inspecting the location of one of the bridge's piers, a ferryboat slammed into the piling Roebling was standing on and crushed his foot. True to his indomitable will, Roebling walked to a doctor's office and ordered the doctor to amputate his toes without an anesthetic. Because of his haste to get back to work, tetanus set in and claimed his life on July 21, 1869. Unfortunately, he never saw his masterpiece completed.

John Roebling revolutionized bridge building with his invention of steel cable.

It [the south tower] was so limber the tower swayed six-teen feet each way. There were a lot of screams all the way to the top. There were twelve or thirteen guys on top, with no way to get down. The elevator wouldn't run. The whole thing would sway toward the ocean, guys would say, "Here we go!" Then it would sway back, to-wards the Bay. Guys were laying on the deck, throwing up and everything. I figured if we go in, the iron would hit the water first.[15]

No damage occurred to the tower. The limberness that the tower displayed in the earthquake was by design, not luck. This flexibility was achieved using two engineering features: the steel cubes that were the basic unit for the steel sections, and the ta-pering of the towers as they rose in height. The base of each of the two legs on each tower began with an area of ninety-seven cells (339.5 square feet) and finished at the top with just twenty-one (73.5 square feet). This tapering was not gradual but, rather, occurred at several intervals. Viewers can see the towers step in as they rise. Strauss, who credited Paine and Morrow for the de-sign, boasted, "This bridge is perhaps the first in which the im-portance of the new motif of stepped-off towers has been recognized and applied."[16] Surviving the earthquake without damage, the south tower was finished with relative ease.

The completion of the twin towers standing against the blue water backdrop of the Pacific illustrated for San Franciscans the power and enormity of the task under way. For the first time, lo-cals and visitors alike came to grips with the scale of the bridge and its place in the history of their city. As they towered above the skyline of San Francisco, civic pride soared. Wide-eyed mer-chant seamen who saw the towers as they departed for interna-tional ports told stories about the construction of the world's largest bridge. Though the majestic towers looked imposing to bystanders, the engineering team knew that they were vulner-able without the cables to help hold them steady.

THE CATWALKS

To kick off the cabling work on August 2, 1935, all shipping through the Gate was closed for the first and only time. At 9:00 A.M., a barge departed from Lime Point on the north side of the Gate and made its way to Fort Point, playing out a 1.5-inch-thick

Construction of the south tower proceeded quickly and with few complications once the pier was completed.

steel guide wire. Minutes after the barge reached Fort Point, derricks, the hoisting devices atop both towers, dropped cables into the water, where workers attached them to the guide wire. The derricks then snapped the glistening guide wire out of the water

RIVETING CREWS

Riveting crews were responsible for joining pieces of steel together with special pins called "rivets." Setting rivets fast enough to keep up with the cranes that were hoisting the steel plates to form the two towers required a team of four well-rehearsed riveters. When the crew was well coordinated and when working conditions were right, a riveting team could set four hundred rivets a day. Rivets begin as steel pins about one inch in diameter, with one end shaped like a mushroom cap measuring about one and a quarter inches.

The process of setting a rivet began with the heater, who was the person responsible for heating the rivets on a charcoal fire. The heater had several different sizes of rivets and would keep several of each type over the coals so that they would be ready to go as soon as the call went out. When the heater got a call for a rivet, he picked one that had a white color, indicating that it was so hot—between 1,000 and 2,000 degrees Fahrenheit—that it was beginning to soften yet still hard enough to maintain its shape. The heater pulled the rivet out of the charcoal with a pair of iron tongs and tossed it through the air to the catcher. The catcher caught the hot rivet in a metal

and hoisted it to the tops of the two towers. The bridgemen cheered the first graceful swoop of line over the channel. With this seemingly simple act, the two sides of the Golden Gate were finally connected.

However, this guide wire would not become a part of the main cables. Instead, it was the first of twenty-five cables used to support two catwalks. The crews would walk on the catwalks while stringing the wires of the two main cables. Ten-foot-wide redwood planking was attached to the guide wires to form the walking platforms. To give some stability to the rather flimsy catwalks in high winds, a web of cables was attached from the towers to the catwalks. In October, the spinning began.

SADDLES AND SPINNING MACHINES

The job of stringing the wires to form the main cables, called

bucket called a "catch bucket," picked it up with tongs, and pushed the narrow end through the two aligned holes of the two pieces of steel being riveted together.

With the hot soft rivet in place, the third man, called the "buckerup," pressed all of his weight against the mushroom-cap end of the rivet with a heavy iron bar called the "colly bar." The riveter then pressed his riveting gun against the narrow end of the rivet and pulled the trigger. This twenty-five-pound gun driven by compressed air, much like a small jackhammer, smacked the rivet with a quick staccato burst until the soft narrow end mushroomed out just like the other end. Both ends of the rivet now had a larger diameter than the hole it was placed in and could not fall out once it had cooled. As soon as one was done, the call went out to the heater for another.

These crews got so good at throwing and catching rivets that they were able to throw them over surprisingly long distances with remarkable accuracy. Accurate throws of thirty to forty feet were common, and throws of up to seventy feet were done when necessary. With dozens of teams riveting at once, competitions emerged to see who could set the fastest pace on the towers.

"spinning," was given to the same company that was supplying the wire—the Roebling Steel Rope Company. They had more experience spinning wire for bridges than any other company. The spinning process was a delicate one requiring each wire to be precise not only in length but also in its downward curve between the two towers. The final and more accurate adjustments were accomplished at the peaks of the towers. Engineers performed final adjustments at night when the cables would be less affected by the warm sunlight which, absorbed by the steel wires, caused them to stretch.

Just as the engineers had had unusual problems to solve when building the two piers, creating the two main cables also required problem-solving skills. Engineers with the Roebling Company had calculated that, as the wires and later the roadway took shape, the unevenness of the weight distribution on the two towers during construction would exert an uneven pull on the tops of the towers, causing them to bend. To eliminate this effect, the Roebling crews installed two large movable steel saddles on the top of each tower over which the wires would run. Set on a carriage of thirty-four 8-inch steel rollers,

Work crews used two catwalks during the construction of the main cables.

A worker stands next to one of the massive saddles used to counteract the uneven stresses exerted on the bridge towers during construction.

each of these massive saddles was 21 feet long, 19 feet wide, and 150 tons. Once in place, the four saddles would glide back and forth on top of the towers to counterbalance the weight as the wires and roadway were added. The saddles adjusted back and forth as much as 66 inches until the span was completed. The saddles would be removed after the completion of the bridge, at which time the cables would be locked into place. Following their lockdown, any stress on the cables would translate to the towers, which had been designed to flex under tension but would always return to their original neutral vertical positions.

A second machine critical for creating the main cables was the spinning machine that looped the lengths of wire from anchorage to anchorage. The machine they designed was a loom-type shuttle that moved back and forth on a heavy guide wire as it strung the cable wires. The shuttle had two wheels, each of which pulled one loop at a time. On November 12, 1935, spinning unceremoniously began with the first two wires, each 0.196 inches in diameter, slightly smaller than a standard wooden pencil. The Roebling Company called these wires their Number 6 cold-drawn, double-galvanized steel bridge wire. Even though they were pencil thin, they were so strong that bridgemen could not bend an eighteen-inch section in half. Calculations had determined that each main cable would require 27,572 of these wires.

SPINNING THE MAIN CABLES

The spinning process of dragging the wire from anchorage to anchorage was technically not a difficult process. Knowing that in-

In order to spin the bridge's main cable, engineers devised a plan to loop wire around the eyebolts in the anchorages.

The spinning machine was a loom-type shuttle that moved back and forth on a guide wire as it strung the main cables.

dividual wires would pull out of the anchorages, engineers devised a plan to loop one continuously running wire around the eyebolts in the anchorages 27,572 times. Here is how the spinning process worked:

To begin, two continuous loops of wire were pulled from a spool at either anchorage and looped around the circumference of a doughnut-shaped "eyebolt shoe," which would later be permanently attached to one of the eyebolts embedded in the concrete anchorage. Next, the spinning machine picked up the two loops, one on each wheel, and spun or dragged them up to the top of the first tower and down to the bottom of the catenary at center span, all the while pulling wire from the huge spool at the anchorage. Then, a spinning wheel from the second tower came down and the wires were transferred over to complete their journey up the second tower and finally to the second anchorage. Upon arriving, the two lengths were looped around the eyebolt shoe and sent back as more wire from the spool played out. This continuous round-trip process repeated itself thousands of times. The total time required to spin two wires from anchorage to anchorage was about fifteen minutes.

What this process meant is that each of the two main cables consists of one 40,000-mile cable continuously looped back and forth, rather than having thousands of individual lengths of wire. Consequently, the spools at each anchorage unrolled the wire in sync with the movement of the spinning machine. However, the Roebling Company did not manufacture one continuous wire 40,000 miles long for each cable. Such a wire would be impossible to manufacture and impossibly heavy to load on a ship. Instead, Roebling manufactured 117,000 coils 3,610 feet long that were spliced together to create the two continuous wires.

Each time 452 wire loops were spun, they were bundled together into a strand, which would later be locked into one of the sixty-one steel eyebolts set deep into the concrete anchorages.

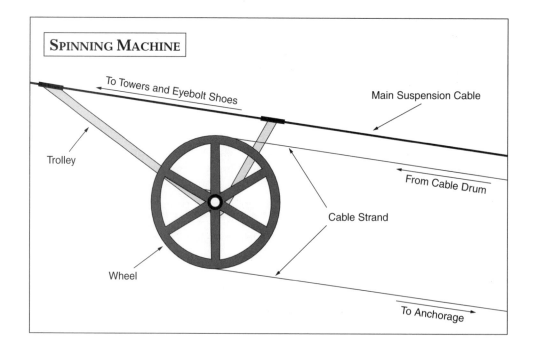

SPINNING MACHINE

To Towers and Eyebolt Shoes

Main Suspension Cable

Trolley

From Cable Drum

Cable Strand

Wheel

To Anchorage

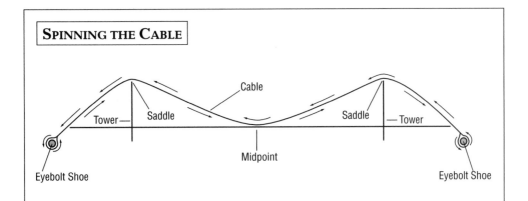

SPINNING THE CABLE

Cable

Tower— Saddle   Saddle —Tower

Eyebolt Shoe   Midpoint   Eyebolt Shoe

The wire was first looped around the eyebolt shoe. Then the spinning wheel pulled the wire over the saddle on the first tower. At the bridge's midpoint, the wire was transferred to the second spinning wheel, which took the wire to the eyebolt shoe at the other end of the bridge, looped it around, and brought the wire back to the midpoint. This process was repeated 27,572 times.

The wires do not wrap around each other in a braid; they all run parallel to each other.

After completing one-third of the spinning, the Roebling Company was well behind schedule, and failure to catch up would cost the company all of its profits. To speed up the spinning, they added a third wheel, allowing them to spin three wires at a time instead of two. It worked perfectly, and soon the crew of 420 spinners was able to spin 1,000 miles of wire a day, or 270 tons. The engineers also increased the speed of the spinning wheels to an amazing 650 feet per minute.

Workers standing on the catwalks inspected each foot of wire for kinks and proper slack. When the wire was in its correct position, the bridgeman gave a hand signal, calling for the next three loops of wire. Standing there was both tedious and dangerous. Alan Brown, in his book *Golden Gate*, writes,

> For the men spinning the giant cables, wind was the worst enemy. In mid-December a forty-mile gale swept through the Golden Gate. Catwalks swung out nearly eight feet from beneath the cable's strands. But, with men stationed at fifty-foot intervals along the catwalks, the spinning wheels continued travelling back and forth across the Golden Gate during the big blow.[17]

Working in thick fog, the bridgemen were often surprised by these spinning wheels. They appeared to come out of nowhere,

MYTHS ABOUT THE MAIN CABLES

The main cables of the Golden Gate Bridge continue to this day to be the objects of public admiration and myth. Many believe that each main cable is one thick cable. Such a cable design would be impossible because no derricks anywhere in the world were powerful enough to hoist a 7,650-foot cable weighing 24,500 tons. Even if such derricks did exist, such a cable would lack the flexibility and strength that are achieved by using many small wires.

Another myth held by many is that the main cables are actually made up of thousands of individual wires. Although this view is closer to the truth, it is only partially correct. It is true that each main cable is made up of 27,572 wires. However, each of these wires is not cut to length and then attached from anchorage to anchorage. Rather, each of these 27,572 wires is one loop of a continuously run wire that is in reality 40,000 miles long.

A third myth is that the individual wires that make up the main cables are braided around each other. They are not. Each was carefully spun so that all would run parallel to the others. This design would make it possible to replace damaged loops, which would not be possible with braided cables.

A cross section of the main cable is displayed near the Golden Gate Bridge.

nearly knocking the men on the catwalks into the bay. To solve this problem, someone decided to attach a cowbell to the wheels so that the men wouldn't be caught off guard.

THE BIG SQUEEZE

On May 20, 1936, two months ahead of schedule, the spinning of the eighty thousand miles of wire required for the two main cables was finished. However, this did not mean that the cables were ready for the roadway; the compression process remained. Compression was accomplished by a machine called a "jack assembly" that had a huge circular clamp that engulfed the entire circumference of each main cable. It traveled along the length of the main cable and compressed the individual strands at the rate of twenty-five feet per hour. The foreman of the jack assembly measured the cable's diameter every few feet, and when each section was precisely 36 ⅜ inches, they moved on to the next section.

Following the cable compression, thin wire was wrapped around the circumference of the entire length of the cable as a protective sheath. The sixty-one bundled strands were then compressed together to form a round cable. The entire length of the cables was compressed except for the last three hundred feet, where each of the individual sixty-one strands was mechanically hooked into the sixty-one iron eyebolts of the anchorages.

HANGING THE SUSPENDER CABLES

The final cabling job was the setting of the five hundred suspender cables that attach the roadway to the two main cables. Engineering studies determined that the final weight of the roadway would require two sets of 2 ¹¹/₁₆-inch suspender cables every fifty feet along each of the main cables. Unlike the main cables, the suspender cables were woven cables like those typically used on cranes. To hold them in place, the suspender cables were attached to the main cables with grooved cast steel saddle bands and then clamped with bolts. The suspender cables were long enough to loop down to the roadway and back up to the saddle bands. Because of the catenary arc of the main cables, the round-trip length of the suspender cables varied from 20 feet at the bottom of the midspan to 980 feet near the two towers.

The five hundred suspender cables, dangling above the water, awaited the last element of the bridge, the roadway. While the construction of the concrete piers and the steel towers presented numerous technical challenges, building the roadway was a standard task. In fact, Strauss planned on building the roadway in essentially the same way that he had for his other suspension bridges. At this point, Strauss and his staff believed that the worst was behind them.

5

VAULTING THE GATE

Finally, after more than three years of setting concrete, steel, and wire, the roadway that would carry commuters and vacationers between Marin and San Francisco was ready for assembly. The roadway did not involve any unusual or complicated technologies, but there was increased danger because of the gaping spaces between the steel beams before the asphalt was added. Strauss, however, always the innovator, was confident that he had a solution in the event that anyone should fall.

EXTENDING THE ROADWAY

To keep the weight of the roadway evenly distributed on the dangling suspender cables, work began simultaneously at each of the two towers and proceeded in both directions, with two crews working toward the north end and two toward the south end. Strauss planned this for two reasons. First, the roadway needed to maintain a careful weight balance as it extended farther and farther away from the towers. If one of the four crews rushed ahead or fell behind the others, the weight imbalance would exert an uneven pull on the cables, stretching them beyond the saddles' ability to adjust. Crews maintained this critical balance by slowing or accelerating the roadway construction from time to time. Finances were the second reason for employing four crews. Working on both sides of both towers meant that four crews would complete the bridge according to the strict timetable and avoid financial penalties for failing to meet the schedule.

Construction began as derricks at the two towers hoisted steel sections up to the 220-foot mark where the roadway was soon to exist. Twenty-five-foot sections of crisscross stiffening trusses that were to be the sides of the roadway were set in place first. As each section arrived, steel posts joined them together. Once the steel posts joined two sections, they were attached to the dangling suspender cables.

To build the roadway, steel sections are hoisted into place and attached to the dangling suspender cables.

AWAITING THE SUN

Every fifty feet, the derricks hoisted up a ninety-foot-wide I beam, called a "cross girder," to join both sides of the roadway. The workers then gave it greater stability by adding diagonal steel braces. As the traveling derricks set the heavy steel, riveting crews secured all of the pieces. In this relatively easy repetitive process, the main roadway steel was set.

As the four sections of the roadway worked toward each other, workers and the public alike became mesmerized by the rapidly approaching completion. However, viewed from a distance and at an angle, the two approaching ends appeared to be misaligned. Many wagered their paychecks predicting the outcome. On September 18, 1936, the *San Francisco Chronicle*

A passenger plane flies over the partially completed Golden Gate Bridge.

printed the banner headline, "The Gap on the Golden Gate Bridge will be closed today."[18]

The last section of steel that would close the center gap was set with Strauss at the controls of the derrick. With cameras recording every move, and San Francisco and the world awaiting this final dramatic moment, grizzled bridgemen who had walked this steel for many years reached out to pull the last beam into place. As the sound of steel banging into steel reverberated across the bay, muscles strained to align the last holes for the rivets, but after several failed attempts the final piece did not fit. It was too short by a whisker.

As a tribute to engineering precision, the final piece needed a few more hours in the sun to warm and expand the few critical millimeters needed for the rivet holes to align. After riveting 1.2 miles of roadway steel, everyone awaited the sun. At just the right moment, at 4:25 in the afternoon, bridgemen set the last large girder, completing the structure of the roadway. As an unknown riveter set the last rivet, he turned to his partner and said, "That's it, Bill."[19]

The steel roadway was now ready for concrete. It would seem that the most dangerous work was now behind the work crews. Such an assumption would be incorrect. Finishing the roadway would bring many different crews together in close quarters, increasing the possibility of injury, or worse, falling.

RISK OF FALLING

Strauss's preoccupation with safety was nowhere more evident than on the roadway construction. He knew that twenty-eight men had fallen during construction of the San Francisco–Oakland Bridge, which had just been completed, and none had survived. A person falling the 220 feet to the water was virtually assured of dying on impact. Hitting water at close to one hundred miles an hour has nearly the same effect as a car traveling at that speed hitting a concrete wall. People who fall into water from these heights usually die from massive internal injuries.

The probability of falling while assembling the roadway was greater than falling while assembling the towers or spinning the cables, because assembling the towers took place from the inside and the catwalks provided reasonable footing for the cable work. Assembling the roadway required the men to work and walk on a latticework of steel beams as narrow as six inches with nothing but several feet of air in between.

To add to the perils of walking the steel beams, the notorious cold gusting winds blowing in from the dark Pacific Ocean often whipped the workmen off balance. Many workmen were struck with terror as their feet suddenly slipped on steel beams slick with the moisture from morning fog or an invisible glaze of ice. This work was not for the faint-hearted, as is evidenced by bridgeman Al Zampa:

> When you're good—only then can you work up in the air like that. They call you aces then, and you're like fighters with fast footwork, quick hands and plenty of guts. You're right up there with the angels, and you're moving all the time. You work with your hands but you're keeping balance with your feet. You have to carry equipment too—wrenches, bolts, sledges—sometimes 30 to 40 pounds of tools. You had to have guts and skill to work high like we did on the Gate job. But I loved every minute of it. It made me feel good to know I was doing something that most guys couldn't.[20]

Concern for the workers' safety prompted Strauss to purchase a huge net that would be tied under the roadway to catch falling workers before they plunged to their deaths. Very much like the nets used in circuses to catch falling trapeze artists, the ⅜-inch-thick hemp net was woven into 6-inch squares. The workmen linked the net to posts that extended ten feet beyond each side of the bridge. Strauss, always the businessman, believed that he could easily recoup the cost of the $125,000 net because the bridgemen would work faster without the fear that they would die if they fell.

The net worked like a charm and saved the lives of many grateful members of the Half Way to Hell Club, a name coined for the workers who had fallen into the net. Much of the work on the roadway required the use of scaffolding to give the men a place to stand to do their work. Generally made of an iron frame with wood planking and clamps, many frames were often stacked 20 to 30 feet high to accommodate crews of up to twenty men. Despite the risks and difficulties of working in winds 220 feet above the water, the men felt safe knowing the net was there.

Unwilling to accept any loss of life during construction, Joseph Strauss installed a net under the roadway to catch fallen workers.

Strauss and his engineering crew were delighted with the progress that the workers were making. Strauss especially appreciated their safety record while setting the steel: Not a single death occurred from falling. Many believed that with the net, no one would take the deadly plunge.

BLACK WEDNESDAY

However, on Wednesday, February 17, 1937, inspectors were summoned to inspect a large section of scaffolding that had been reported as looking suspicious. As the inspectors were making their way toward the scaffolding in question, they froze in their steps at an ear-splitting sound unlike anything they had ever heard. Slim Lambert, the foreman of the crew on the scaffolding, recalled in an interview with the *San Francisco Chronicle*,

> I felt the stripper [scaffolding] give a funny shudder, then it lurched to one side. I shouted and without waiting I jumped. I must have acted instinctively, because I don't remember thinking. I landed in the net. A moment later I heard a sound like thunder as the stripper ripped from its hangers.[21]

THE HALF WAY TO HELL CLUB

In the early 1930s, the Golden Gate Bridge was the latest in a long history of great bridges built in America. However, along with building a great structure comes danger and the chance of death. Statistically, bridge builders calculated "acceptable loss of life" to be equal to one man for every $1 million spent. The Golden Gate Bridge had a price tag of close to $35 million. Strauss did not find thirty-five deaths acceptable, so he set out to build a bridge with zero tolerance for death.

Of all the safety regulations and safety devices that Strauss required, none gained more attention from the bridgemen than the great net that extended the entire length of the underbelly of the roadway. Just like circus nets, it would catch falling men.

The net worked as expected. A total of nineteen men fell into the net and were fished out with a whoop by the other bridgemen. Anyone who returned to work after having fallen into the net automatically became a proud member of the Half Way to Hell Club. Jumping into the net for fun, as a few enjoyed doing, did not qualify for the club.

Although the net was built to catch falling men, it also caught all manner of tools and material. Once a week the bridge foremen would send the young apprentice workers in to the net to clean it out and many of them volunteered for the weekly clean-up. The net could also be fun. Many of the young men enjoyed bouncing along the net as if playing on a trampoline 220 feet above the water.

Rushing to the side of the bridge, the inspection team, along with dozens of bridgemen, watched in horror as the five-ton section of scaffolding and the thirteen men standing on it collapsed into the net. When the scaffolding hit the net, it paused for an instant before tearing through the six-inch squares, sending men and scaffolding spilling into the bay. A bridge painter who saw the sequence of events said that "The net cracked like a machine gun," and another added, "Then it ripped like a picket fence splintering."[22] Several bridgemen who witnessed the tragedy unfold described it as though it took place in slow mo-

SAFETY

Workers' safety during the construction of the bridge went far beyond Strauss's famous net. In addition to the risk of death from falling, the workers faced other possible injuries on the project. Strauss established a number of safety precautions to protect the bridgemen.

Injuries from falling debris prompted Strauss to order all workers to wear hard hats. Not entirely revolutionary, it was nonetheless a first for a bridge project, and hard hats saved many from serious head injury, if not death. In addition to hard hats, Strauss required all ironworkers and riveters to wear leather gloves to prevent them from being burned by the hot steel. For those who worked in the air, safety belts called "tie-off lines" were provided; they looped around steel beams or were clipped to wire handrails. Problems with sun glare reflecting off the water prompted Strauss to require the use of sun goggles and even sunscreen lotions to keep men on the job.

To treat more serious injuries and illness such as the epidemic of lead poisoning, Strauss established a field hospital at the south end of the Gate that was staffed on a full-time basis. The hospital treated twelve thousand injuries by the end of 1935. The most common injuries were cuts and bruises from falling tools and material. Back and neck strains were also common as a result of lifting heavy loads.

Remarkably, despite a workforce averaging thirteen hundred men each day, no man died on the project for the

tion. They recalled the screams of the falling men sounding like the cries of babies. One man managed to grab the net in midair and tried climbing it, but the entire net was ripped away from the bridge and his valiant attempt became futile. In five seconds, twenty-one hundred feet of net had been ripped away and was left dangling in the water.

Only three of the thirteen men who fell survived what has become known as Black Wednesday. One of the men survived the fall by grabbing onto steel rails on the way down. Another recovered in the hospital after suffering a fractured hip, a broken

To protect workers, Strauss implemented a number of safety rules, including the use of gloves and hard hats.

first three years and eight months. However, on October 21, 1936, Kermit Moore was tragically decapitated by a falling crane. As had always been the tradition among bridgemen, all work halted and the entire crew took the remainder of the day off.

Safety was sometimes jeopardized by drunkenness and showing off. Strauss refused to tolerate either. Workers drunk on the job were fired. The same held true for workers competing with each other to see who could walk steel beams with their eyes closed, walk backwards, or recklessly jump from one beam to another hundreds of feet above the water.

leg, and serious internal injuries. The third, Slim Lambert, the foreman, was remarkably uninjured. In his interview with the *San Francisco Chronicle*, he recalled from his hospital bed,

> As I drifted with the tide, I saw three pairs of feet sticking out of the water. I don't know whose they were. I watched them and tried to make my way over to where they were, but I couldn't buck the tide. Then they disappeared one pair at a time. I closed my eyes for a while, then looked up. About four feet away from me was the face of a man I knew. It was like paste. I tried to swim towards it. Then a terrible expression crossed the face. I knew the man was dead. He sank before my eyes.[23]

Lambert eventually drifted out of the Gate. Although he thought that he would soon die, a fishing boat that had witnessed the catastrophe came by and hauled him in.

The man who had grabbed a girder before falling was found hanging with his pipe still in his mouth. Workers hollered to him to hang on as they lowered a rope to pull him back up to the roadway. However, he was frozen in terror and refused to release his grip as he dangled and twisted in the winds with nothing between him and the water. Finally, a harness was looped around him and four men pulled him to safety, still holding on to his pipe with his teeth. Frenchy Gales, one of the men who witnessed this rescue, recalled in an interview with John Van Der Zee that the man with the pipe "walked down to the Field Office, picked up his time [paycheck], and never came back."[24]

Following the accident, investigations were conducted to determine who was at fault for this tragedy. After several days of investigative hearings, the matter was dismissed, and work on the bridge resumed at a slower and more cautious pace. The net was replaced within a month. Although many people blamed him for the accident, Strauss felt that it was not his fault. In fact, he said that his net had already saved many lives.

Strauss and the entire bridge crew were inconsolable for months after the accident, which continues to mar the history of the Golden Gate Bridge to this day. Despite the tragic event, the crews knew that the schedule for completion of the bridge would not be extended and they had to move forward.

FINISHING TOUCHES

Now that all of the structural steel had been set, engineers were ready to make the finishing touches on the bridge. They would add the concrete road, the pedestrian walkway, the curbs, lighting, paint, and myriad other details to get the bridge ready for

Finishing touches such as lights, curbs, a guardrail, and a walkway were added to the completed bridge.

FATAL ATTRACTION

 When Joseph Strauss and his team designed the bridge rails, one of their concerns was suicide prevention. For centuries, people intent on taking their lives have been drawn to bridges and other places of beauty and elegance for their last moments. In the case of the Golden Gate Bridge, the jump is easy to make because of the accessible walkway, the relatively low guardrail, and the virtual guarantee of death.

The first jump occurred three months after the opening of the bridge. A San Franciscan was walking and talking with a complete stranger when he abruptly handed his coat and vest to the man and said, "This is as far as I go." Within a year, the number had shot up to ten and it became clear to everyone that the Golden Gate Bridge had become a magnet for those intent on ending their lives. More than half who commit suicide there leave a note describing some form of depression in their lives. By the time the bridge's fiftieth anniversary had arrived, the recorded number of recovered bodies had reached 840.

Today, suicide prevention remains a concern for the bridge directors. Security guards viewing television monitors have stopped many jumpers in time to save their lives. Many citizens believe that higher guardrails could reduce the number of deaths. Nonetheless, California law does not prohibit suicide, and the beautiful Golden Gate Bridge continues to exert a fatal attraction for many each year.

opening day. They used the traveling derricks to lay the lighter steel beams that would support the roadway, curbs, walkways, and guardrails.

Construction workers poured the roadway over sheets of corrugated metal in three long ribbons of concrete the length of the bridge. The two outer ribbons were poured first in 20-by-50-foot sections, and once they had been completed, workers filled in the middle ribbon. The combined width of the road was 62 feet, and the concrete was poured to a depth of 5 inches. Next, the pedestrian sidewalks on both sides of the bridge were poured to a width of 10.5 feet.

At this point in the construction process, the main cables were supporting close to the final weight of the bridge, except for cars and a few incidental elements. Engineers measured the lengths of the main cables and found that they had actually increased by twenty-one feet as a result of stretching under their own weight and the weight of the roadway.

To prevent pedestrians from wandering over the edge of the bridge, a guardrail was needed. The guardrail was the subject of great debate because of both aesthetics and its ability to prevent suicides. Though it was originally designed by Strauss to be five feet six inches high to prevent suicide attempts, designers reduced the height to three feet six inches to improve the view for pedestrians and motorists. The designers also believed that people who wanted to commit suicide would find a way over the rail regardless of its height or would find another bridge or high building.

Suicide prevention was the primary social concern for the citizens of San Francisco, and lighting was their primary aesthetic concern. Consulting architect Irving F. Morrow envisioned a bejeweled ornament sparkling in the night light. Because of the bridge's great size, Morrow did not want the same intensity of light on all parts of the bridge because that would seem too artificial. The towers, for example, were to have less light at the top so that they would seem to soar beyond the range of illumination.

Unfortunately, the tower lighting originally envisioned by Morrow was not installed during the construction of the bridge because of budgetary constraints. However, shortly after its fiftieth anniversary, the bridge towers came to life with light. Just as Morrow had envisioned, with the new lighting the towers seemed to disappear into the evening darkness, further accenting their great height.

Because of the scale and dignity of the bridge, Morrow also believed that tricky, flashy, or spectacular lighting would be unworthy of the structure's magnificence. Thus, he selected low-pressure sodium vapor lamps with a subtle amber glow for the roadway, which provided warm, nonglare lighting for passing motorists. The lamps were the most modern available in 1937.

In addition to the lighting that has dazzled and entertained visitors and San Franciscans, functional lighting was added to provide safety for commuters. The functional lighting includes

128 roadway lights, 24 sidewalk lights around both towers, and 8 lights on each main cable.

The least significant bridge element, the paint, received far more attention than was probably warranted. Everyone understood that without a protective coating of paint, the corrosive effects of the salt air would quickly rust through the steel of the bridge. The debate that raged surrounded the color.

PAINTING THE BRIDGE

The sole purpose for painting the bridge was to place a protective coating on the steel to prevent rust and corrosion caused by the high salt content in the air and water. Many misconceptions exist about how the bridge is painted and

Two workers paint the Golden Gate Bridge.

The navy believed that the bridge would be most noticeable in the fog if it were painted with broad stripes of alternating gray and yellow. Many were horrified by this recommendation, and solid gray and an orange-red color became the final two candidates. The final decision was made by Morrow, who selected the reddish orange, called "international orange," as the best visual choice. It is the color that is still used today.

how often. Some say it is painted once every seven years; others say from end-to-end each year. Actually, the Golden Gate Bridge has been painted in its entirety only one time, and that was when it was originally built.

For twenty-seven years, only touch-ups were required. But by 1968, advancing corrosion resulted in a program to remove the original paint and replace it with an improved paint. Years later, in 1990, the top-coat was changed to acrylic emulsion to meet air-quality requirements. Although the program was completed in 1995, there are continuous touch-ups on areas with severe erosion. Painting the bridge is an ongoing task and is the bridge's primary maintenance job, consuming more money annually than any other maintenance activity.

The job has changed little over the years; however, modern tools and machinery now assist the thirty-eight full-time painters. Unlike with the first painters, rust is now removed by sandblasting instead of chipping, and paintbrushes have largely given way to high-pressure paint guns. Scaffolding that was once worked by pulling on ropes is now automated, providing effortless rides up and down the towers. To prevent dripping international orange on cars, the mobile scaffolding is covered in heavy tarps.

Safety, always an important consideration, forbids painting when the winds are gusting, and over the years, only two painters have lost their lives while painting the bridge, both from tragic falls.

COLLISION PREVENTION

One of the concerns expressed by those debating the color and lighting of the bridge was the possibility that ships and aircraft might fail to see the bridge and collide with it. The bridge was built right in the middle of one of the busiest and narrowest shipping channels in the world. Addressing this concern, engineers outfitted the bridge with warning lights and foghorns to warn planes and ships of its position in the channel.

To prevent planes from colliding with the bridge, the top of each tower was originally fitted with a red rotating aircraft beacon. This was replaced in 1980 with a modern flashing red beacon that emits light in all directions. The main cables have red lights to notify night-flying pilots of the main cables and suspender cables. No aircraft has ever struck the bridge.

The greater risk of collision came from ships since the south pier supporting the south tower sits eleven hundred feet into the narrow channel. To warn ships, engineers placed red navigation lights on the pier fender and white and green lights below the roadway at midspan. These actions have proved successful, since no ships have sunk as a result of colliding with the fender. However, from time to time freighters in dense fog or turbulent waters have been known to strike it.

To complement the lights, which are often invisible to ship captains in the fog, engineers placed two foghorns on the bridge, one at midspan and one at the south pier. Operated by compressed air, their baritone sounds have guided hundreds of thousands of vessels safely past the south pier. Small vessels that do not have radar still use the bridge foghorns as guides when visibility in the Golden Gate Strait is low. Each horn has a different pitch, and marine navigational charts provide the frequency, or signature, of each foghorn. Their unmistakable deep tones, announcing the arrival of the fog, have also become a favorite sound to San Franciscans and are one of the unique features of their city. They operate, on average, two and a half hours a day, but during the Bay Area's foggy season, July through October, they sound continuously for more than five hours a day.

THE GOLDEN RIVET

With all of the finishing details completed, the time had arrived for speeches and the final ceremony commemorating the com-

After more than four years of construction, the Golden Gate Bridge was completed in 1937.

pletion of the bridge. On April 27, 1937, with the official public grand opening still a month away, a quiet ceremony celebrating the completion of the bridge was held for a small number of officials who had been actively involved with the building of the bridge and a few invited guests. The key moment was to be the setting of the last rivet, which was made of gold mined in California's gold country. Of interest to everyone was the way officials linked this historic event with others in the short history of the West and California. One guest, Joseph Graham, had witnessed the driving of the golden spike during the ceremony celebrating the completion of the Transcontinental Railroad in 1869 at Promontory, Utah. Another, J. H. P. Gedge, one of the original 49ers, had sailed through the Golden Gate in 1849 at the height of the famous California gold rush that had thrust San Francisco and California into greatness. Both references were fitting.

At the ceremony, as everyone gathered around the gleaming rivet, two specially chosen riveters stepped forward to complete the job. Gold, much softer than the usual steel, proved to be a glamorous idea but not a practical one. After a couple of raps from the riveting hammer, the head of the gold rivet fell off. The riveters then tried to extract the remainder of the rivet and that too fell into the bay. Since no one could retrieve either part of the gold rivet, much to the embarrassment of the prominent officials, they finally set a steel one. The bridge was now ready for the citizens of San Francisco.

OPENING DAY

On May 27, 1937, the big day finally arrived. The first of several days of celebration, this one was strictly for pedestrians only. It was a magical celebration for many of the people. Every imaginable type of entertainment had been planned, from President Roosevelt signaling the official opening of the bridge with a flash of light, to marching bands, warships, and speeches from Strauss and city dignitaries.

At 6:00 A.M., as the foghorns let loose with a blast announcing the official public opening of the bridge, thousands of early arrivers scurried across the bridge in both directions. Everyone wanted to be the first to cross it in some special way. One woman crossed both directions on stilts, another woman crossed sticking her tongue out the entire distance, a couple roller-skated across, one man blew a tuba across, while another did the route walking backwards. Two teenage boys crawled on to the net and were trying to bounce their way across it but guards intercepted them and pulled them off. Everyone wanted to do something memorable, something for the record books.

Thousands of people run across the Golden Gate Bridge moments after it was opened to the public on May 27, 1937.

At 10:00, the great man himself, Joseph Strauss, appeared to make his very short speech. The rest of the day was given over to the merrymaking of people enjoying the seemingly magical feat that had finally taken place. By afternoon, the winds of the Gate whipped up and blew hundreds of colorful festive hats off the heads of fashionable men and women, sailing them over the bridge like handfuls of confetti. The famous net that had saved so many lives yet had given up ten in one tragic moment caught hundreds of purses, hats, and other articles of clothing lost by the celebrants. By day's end, an estimated 200,000 revelers had marked the historic event with their presence. To this day, many old-timers still enjoy talking about the day as one of the peak experiences of their lives.

EPILOGUE

After more than sixty years of nearly uninterrupted service, the Golden Gate Bridge stands and looks today exactly as it did on opening day. In terms of service to the citizens of San Francisco and the world, it has been remarkably loyal. Battered by every force of nature known to inhabit this cosmopolitan corner of the world, it has never faltered.

The most remarkable tribute to the bridge is the number of cars that have safely crossed its span. Built to replace the old unreliable, slow, and accident-prone ferryboats, the bridge has succeeded beyond the expectations of its builders. This link between San Francisco and Marin County is a significant contribution to the greater San Francisco metropolitan area. The second most remarkable tribute to the bridge is as San Francisco's most endearing landmark. Recognized throughout the world, it has been one of the city's primary tourist attractions over the years. It is also a favorite attraction for the locals, most of whom know its history.

On May 24, 1987, eight hundred thousand people crowded onto the Golden Gate Bridge to celebrate its fiftieth anniversary.

For these facts, we have the engineering talent of Strauss and his staff to thank. They demanded precise attention to detail, a willingness to work late into many nights, and the strength to press forward with the courage of their convictions.

THE FIFTIETH ANNIVERSARY CELEBRATION

The dream of spanning the Golden Gate Strait had been around for many years before the Golden Gate Bridge opened to pedestrians on May 27, 1937. On Sunday, May 24, 1987, this dream come true was celebrated as the Golden Gate Bridge turned fifty. With great fanfare, people from all over the world came to pay homage to the bridge and become part of a historical celebration.

The celebration was called "Bridgewalk '87," a reenactment of "Pedestrian Day '37." The day began, as it had in 1937, with the opening of the great span to pedestrians only. From both ends of the bridge, an estimated 300,000 people surged onto the roadway at the sound of the foghorn. From both the north and the south these two groups ran, danced, and frolicked their way toward the center, where they came to a standstill because of the density of the crowd. This concentration of people was the heaviest weight ever placed on the bridge, and to the dismay of bridge engineers and citizens alike, the slight upward arc in the center of the roadway flattened out.

By 11:00 A.M., the roadway was cleared of the revelers to make way for a commemorative vintage automobile motorcade. Vintage cars in pristine condition motored across the bridge to the cheers of those standing on the two walkways. As a token of appreciation to the thousands of motorists who use the bridge each day, the board of directors suspended toll collection for the remainder of the day when normal traffic resumed.

By afternoon, everyone adjourned to Crissy Field, a beautiful grassy field near the south end of the bridge, where speeches were followed by music, food fests, and fireworks after sunset. Estimated by many to have been the most elaborate in the history of San Francisco, the grand finale featured a pyrotechnic waterfall cascading over the east rail of the bridge into the dark waters of the bay.

They built the bridge that so many said couldn't be built. We also have the construction crews to thank for their willingness to risk their lives on a daily basis to implement the dreams of the engineers. Working during the Great Depression to connect earth to concrete and concrete to steel, these almost superhumans burrowed in mud, seawater, and concrete to prepare the way for those who would "walk the air." No one understood their contribution better than Joseph Strauss, who eulogized them in this way:

> There is an ancient saying about bridgemen that the bridge demands its life. Among modern builders, the rule of thumb is one life for every million dollars' worth of construction. That seems an appalling sacrifice, and one would think it next to impossible to find men to take the risk. But the very reverse is true. Bridgemen are a breed unto themselves. There are always more men seeking work than there are jobs, just as there are always more men than are needed to fight a war.[25]

Notes

Chapter 1: The Bridge That Couldn't Be Built

1. *San Francisco Bulletin*, editorial page, August 26, 1916.
2. Quoted in John Van Der Zee, *Gate: The True Story of the Design and Construction of the Golden Gate Bridge*. New York: Simon and Schuster, 1986, p. 47.
3. Quoted in Charles F. Adams, *Heroes of the Golden Gate*. Palo Alto, CA: Pacific Books, 1987, p. 83.

Chapter 2: Engineering a Dream

4. Quoted in Alan Brown, *Golden Gate: Biography of a Bridge*. Garden City, NY: Doubleday, 1965, p. 116.
5. Quoted in Van Der Zee, *Gate*, p. 101.
6. Quoted in Van Der Zee, *Gate*, p. 127.

Chapter 3: Deep Roots

7. Quoted in James W. Schock, *The Bridge: A Celebration*. Mill Valley, CA: Golden Gate International, 1997, p. 7.
8. Quoted in Van Der Zee, *Gate,* pp. 181–82.
9. Adams, *Heroes of the Golden Gate*, p. 163.
10. Quoted in Van Der Zee, *Gate*, p. 175.
11. Stephen Cassady, *Spanning the Gate: The Golden Gate Bridge*. Mill Valley, CA: Squarebooks, 1986, p. 51.
12. Quoted in Cassady, *Spanning the Gate*, p. 7.
13. Quoted in Schock, *The Bridge*, p. 6.

Chapter 4: High Steel

14. Van Der Zee, *Gate*, p. 107.
15. Quoted in Van Der Zee, *Gate*, p. 224.
16. Quoted in Schock, *The Bridge*, p. 56.
17. Brown, *Golden Gate*, p. 98.

Chapter 5: Vaulting the Gate

18. *San Francisco Chronicle*, front page, September 18, 1936.
19. Quoted in Brown, *Golden Gate*, p. 106.
20. Quoted in Cassady, *Spanning the Gate*, p. 103.

21. Quoted in *San Francisco Chronicle*, February 18, 1937.

22. Quoted in *San Francisco Chronicle*, February 18, 1937.

23. Quoted in *San Francisco Chronicle*, February 18, 1937.

24. Quoted in Van Der Zee, *Gate*, p. 237.

Epilogue
25. Quoted in Cassady, *Spanning the Gate*, p. 65.

FOR FURTHER READING

Highlights, Facts, and Figures. San Francisco: Golden Gate Highway and Transportation District, 2000. This small book has been compiled by nontechnical employees and members of the engineering staff of the Golden Gate Bridge. It provides a history of bridge construction and information about bridge repair and modernization. It is a simple yet comprehensive book with many black-and-white photos.

David McCullough, *The Great Bridge: The Epic Story of the Building of the Brooklyn Bridge.* New York: Simon and Schuster, 1983. This book discusses many of the engineering problems that builders of the Golden Gate Bridge also encountered. A reading of this book reveals insight into the construction of suspension bridges and introduces the reader to the Roebling family who provided the steel cables for both the Brooklyn and the Golden Gate Bridges. The author also discusses the economics and politics of building the bridge.

E. Cromwell Menfsch, *Golden Gate Bridge: Technical Description in Ordinary Language.* San Francisco: Golden Gate Highway and Transportation District, 1935. A superb collection of architectural drawings and relatively simple and clean discussions of most major engineering challenges. Because it was published prior to the completion of the Golden Gate Bridge, there are no photos.

Kathy Pelta, *Bridging the Golden Gate.* Minneapolis, MN: Lerner, 1987. This is a well-written chronological history of the building of the Golden Gate Bridge written for a junior high audience. It provides a good mix of engineering and anecdotal material and is illustrated with black-and-white photographs.

WORKS CONSULTED

Charles F. Adams, *Heroes of the Golden Gate*. Palo Alto, CA: Pacific Books, 1987. This book presents an excellent history of the building of the Golden Gate Bridge. The large number of interviews with many who worked on the bridge adds to the authenticity of the story. Adams also interviews other figures who lend insight into the personalities and politics of the project.

Alan Brown, *Golden Gate: Biography of a Bridge*. Garden City, NY: Doubleday, 1965. Brown provides an excellent chronological study of the engineering and construction of the Golden Gate Bridge. This book contains many quotes from and stories about the engineering staff and the bridge workers.

Stephen Cassady, *Spanning the Gate: The Golden Gate Bridge*. Mill Valley, CA: Squarebooks, 1986. This book on the Golden Gate Bridge strikes one of the best balances between technical data, unusual photographs of construction, and lively interviews with the builders and engineers.

Tom Horton and Baron Wolman, *Superspan: The Golden Gate Bridge*. San Francisco: Chronicle Books, 1983. *Superspan*, like many of the books chronicling the building of the Golden Gate Bridge, presents a very good history of its construction. Its real strength is the presentation of many beautiful photographs of the bridge.

Richard Thomas Loomis, *The History of the Building of the Golden Gate Bridge*. Ann Arbor, MI: International Microfilm, 1959. This book is a Ph.D. thesis on the bridge that provides a glimpse into the administrative, political, and sociological issues surrounding the bridge.

James W. Schock, *The Bridge: A Celebration*. Mill Valley, CA: Golden Gate International, 1997. James Schock wrote this book to commemorate the building of the Golden Gate Bridge. Though it does not delve into the technical issues of construction as much as other books on the bridge do, it does include a great deal of material on the opening day celebration, excellent photographs, and an informative year-by-year history of the bridge from 1937 through 1996.

These year-by-year history highlights include excerpts from the annual report such as maintenance issues, maintenance costs, unusual occurrences, and the historical highlights for each year.

Joseph B. Strauss, *The Golden Gate Bridge: Report of the Chief Engineer to the Board of Directors of the Golden Gate Bridge and Highway District with Architectural Studies.* San Francisco: Golden Gate Bridge and Highway District, 1938. This book provides most of the definitive technical descriptions, drawings, and computations that were used to describe the bridge to the Golden Gate Bridge and Highway District that managed the construction. Most of the good books written about the Golden Gate Bridge use this for engineering details.

John Van Der Zee, *Gate: The True Story of the Design and Construction of the Golden Gate Bridge.* New York: Simon and Schuster, 1986. This book is one of the more detailed in terms of technical accomplishment and the politics of building and financing the Golden Gate Bridge. Van Der Zee provides an excellent backdrop to the events and political forces at work in the San Francisco area from the turn of the century through the Great Depression.

INDEX

PICTURE CREDITS

ABOUT THE AUTHOR

James Barter received his undergraduate degree in history and classics at the University of California at Berkeley. He followed this with graduate studies at the University of Pennsylvania and a Fulbright Scholarship at the American Academy in Rome. Mr. Barter has taught European history as well as Latin and Greek.

Mr. Barter grew up in the picturesque hills of Berkeley overlooking the fabled San Francisco Bay and fondly remembers watching the flashing red lights of the Golden Gate Bridge and listening to his parents, Cy and Martha, talk about their cherished memories of opening day on the bridge.

Mr. Barter lives in Rancho Santa Fe, California, and has two daughters, Kalista, who is a sophomore at Torrey Pines High School, and Tiffany, who is a classical violinist with the Kansas City Symphony.